JAMES

WESLEY BIBLE STUDIES

wphonline.com

Copyright © 2014 by Wesleyan Publishing House
Published by Wesleyan Publishing House
Indianapolis, Indiana 46250
Printed in the United States of America
ISBN: 978-0-89827-840-8
ISBN (e-book): 978-0-89827-841-5

CONTENTS

Introduction   5

1. The Value of Life's Trials
   James 1:1–8   8

2. The Giver of Perfect Gifts
   James 1:9–18   16

3. Do the Word
   James 1:19–27   25

4. The Royal Law
   James 2:1–13   33

5. Complete Faith
   James 2:14–26   41

6. The Power to Bless
   James 3:1–12   51

7. Two Ways of Thinking
   James 3:13–18   59

8. A Genuine Heart Change
   James 4:1–10   67

9. A Wiser Way to Live
   James 4:11–17   75

10. The Problem with Money
    James 5:1–6   81

11. The Wisdom of Patience
    James 5:7–12   88

12. The Power of Prayer
    James 5:13–20   97

Words from Wesley Works Cited   105

INTRODUCTION

Faith and . . .

Sola fide. Those Latin words became a rallying cry for the reformers of the sixteenth century. Long burdened by legalistic requirements that called upon Christians to earn salvation by good works, reformers like Martin Luther found freedom in the biblical truth that salvation from sin is obtained by *faith alone*. Not surprisingly, some of these same leaders were troubled by the writings of James, whose letter is filled with references to faith but places a corresponding emphasis on actions. Rather than seeing faith as the end of the journey, James views it as the beginning. Seeing the inextricable link between our thoughts and actions, James chooses to emphasize what he sees as the logical result of faith—changed behavior. James states, "Faith without deeds is dead" (James 2:26). It is no wonder that this little book has been ignored by some Christians, including Luther, who famously referred to it as an "epistle of straw."

Indeed, the book of James is challenging, for the author refused to allow Christians to sit still in their relationship with Christ. James constantly pushes believers go further, grow deeper, and strengthen what faith they already have. For James, faith is good. Yet he, like Peter (see 2 Pet. 1:5–9), urge us through their letters to add virtues to it. In James we read not *faith alone*, but *faith and*.

FAITH AND ENDURANCE

Few biblical writers deal as straightforwardly with the issue of suffering as does James. His classic advice to "consider it pure joy" when suffering trials is both often quoted and often ignored. James insists that faith must naturally grow into perseverance if we are to mature. This letter insists that facing difficulties develops and stabilizes our faith and that God provides for the personal and spiritual needs of each individual regardless of what we suffer. James does not coddle believers with the notion that failure is normal in these trying times of ours. Instead, believers are urged to embrace suffering as a means of developing an even stronger faith and lifestyle. Don't settle for merely accepting the notion that God is good. Live as if you believe it is true, would be James' advice.

FAITH AND ACTION

There is a direct relationship between what we believe and what we do. Most of us understand that. We know that belief affects behavior. James tersely advises Christians that their lifestyle is a clear indicator of their faith. The implication is that those who claim to have faith but act in ways contrary to the gospel are really kidding themselves. Faith alone, if not accompanied by appropriate action, is worthless. In James we find some of the classic biblical texts that urge Christians to "walk the talk."

FAITH AND LOVE

There is perhaps no better measure of our faith than the result it produces in our relationships with others. Much of the practical advice in James bears directly on this point. If we believe what we say about God's love for us, that should result in improved relationships with others. We will keep our words in check so we don't harm others by gossip or hurtful talk. We will treat others fairly, not showing favoritism to the rich or slighting the poor. We will pray for one another. James sees our personal ethics as a litmus test for our profession of faith. If we love God, we will love others.

FAITH AND WISDOM

With its emphasis on practical living, the book of James has much in common with the Wisdom Literature of the Old Testament, particularly Proverbs. For James, living by faith boils down to a series of everyday actions. Faith means being tolerant of others, reserving judgment about the future, and avoiding the entanglement of loving money. We hear in James a direct echo of the teachings on practical living that Jesus set forth in His Sermon on the Mount (see Matt. 5–7).

Christians believe that Jesus is alive. If this is the case, James might ask, "Are you acting like it?"

THE VALUE OF LIFE'S TRIALS

James 1:1–8

Facing difficulties develops and stabilizes our faith.

What's going on in your life right now? Chances are good that you are facing a mix of circumstances, including some that are pleasurable and others that are painful. Jesus said the rain falls on the righteous and unrighteous alike (Matt. 5:45). We all suffer, like it or not. And most of us don't like it.

James puts our trials into a new light. Rather than problems to be lamented, they may be seen as opportunities to be embraced. This study will help you gain a new perspective on your circumstances and see that God is constantly at work in your life, even when it doesn't turn out the way you expected.

COMMENTARY

The book of James is reminiscent of the Old Testament Wisdom Literature. Like a string of beads, one teaching or exhortation follows another with little or no transition. Most of the topics addressed by James are introduced in the first chapter in rapid sequence. Then they are examined further in what appears to be random order—sometimes more than once.

James is a very practical book that emphasizes the need to care for the needy, avoid showing favoritism to the rich, and put God's Word into action in every area of life. There is very little theological foundation made for these practical teachings. Jesus is mentioned only twice, and His resurrection is not mentioned at all. In fact, the author emphasized works so much that Martin

Luther thought James contradicted the writings of Paul. This has led some throughout church history to question its acceptance as God's Word.

However, there is no reason to think of James as a second-class epistle. There are several similarities between the teachings of James and Peter, James and Paul, and even James and Jesus. Consider these similarities between the teachings of James and Jesus. Both teach that believing is the key to answered prayer (James 1:5–8; Matt. 21:18–22; Mark 11:20–24). Jesus tells us not to judge others, as does James (James 4:11–12; Matt. 7:1; Luke 6:37). Both tell us to humble ourselves (James 4:10; Matt. 23:12). Jesus and James both tell us not to swear (James 5:12; Matt. 5:34–37). James' emphasis on hearing and doing God's Word echoes Jesus' teaching (James 1:25; Matt. 5:17–20; 7:21, 24–27; Luke 11:28; John 13:17). Both consider poverty a blessing and wealth a danger (James 1:9–11; Matt. 19:23–24; Luke 6:20–23). Jesus and James both say that sin comes out of the heart (James 1:13–15; Matt. 15:17–20). Both teachers say that mercy will be shown to the merciful (James 2:13; Matt. 5:7). They teach that anger is sin (James 1:19–20; Matt. 5:21–22). They condemn loving the world (James 4:4; John 15:18–25). Jesus and James both remind us that God will judge us (James 4:12; Matt. 10:28).

There are also a few similarities between James and the first letter of Peter. Both books say God gives us new birth (James 1:18; 1 Pet. 1:3). They both command Christians to resist the Devil (James 4:7; 1 Pet. 5:8–9). They also both remind us of the need to humble ourselves before God and that He will exalt us when we do (James 4:10; 1 Pet. 5:6).

In spite of the supposed contradictions when comparing the book of James and the letters of Paul, several parallels do exist—even on the topic of faith and works. These writings commend the benefits of suffering (James 1:3; Rom. 5:3). They insist that justification comes to those who hear and obey (James 1:22; Rom. 2:13). James and Paul's letters recognize the Christian's inner struggle with sin (James 1:14; Rom. 7:23). Both writings ask us: Who are you to judge another? (James 4:12; Rom. 14:4). They point out that sin leads to death (James 1:15; Rom. 6:15–18). Paul's letters and the book of James tell us that faith must change the way we act (James 2:14–26; Rom. 1:5; Gal. 5:6; Eph. 2:8–10). They call on Christians to avoid showing favoritism (James 2:1–11; 1 Tim. 5:21). They call us to be careful about our views of wealth (James 1:9–11; 5:1–6; 1 Tim. 6:6–19). James and Paul's letters tell us to keep the royal law of love (James 2:8–11; Rom. 13:8–10; Gal. 5:13–14).

There really are no contradictions between the writings of James and Paul, only different emphases. Paul wrote to correct an error in teaching that led Jews and Gentiles to believe they could be justified by following the Old Testament laws. He called us to trust in Jesus' death and resurrection alone for salvation, reminding us that "we are God's workmanship, created in Christ Jesus to do good works, which God prepared in advance for us to do" (Eph. 2:10). James wrote to Jewish believers who seem to think that merely believing the right doctrines is all that is involved in salvation. He challenged this heresy by asking, "Do you believe there is one God? Good! Even the demons believe that—and they shudder at the thought of Him! What does your faith make you do?" Each writer called us to live out Jesus' teachings *because* we are saved, not *in order to be* saved.

The Address (James 1:1)

Who was **James**? There were several men called James in the New Testament. However, only three were considered apostles: James, the brother of John (the son of Zebedee); James, the son of Alphaeus; and James, the brother of Jesus (Matt. 4:21–22; 10:2–4; 13:55). Of these three, only James, the brother of John, and James, the brother of Jesus, were leaders in the church at Jerusalem. James, the son of Zebedee, was the first apostle to die for his faith (Acts 12:2), so he could not have written this letter. James, the brother of Jesus, was the pastor of the Jerusalem church. It was to this James that Peter sent word when the angel released him from prison (Acts 12:17). Paul reported what he had been preaching to "James, the Lord's brother" (Gal. 1:18–19). This James suggested the answer to the question about how Jewish the Gentile Christians needed to become (Acts 15:12–21). James, the brother of Jesus, was martyred around A.D. 62, so the book must have been written before that.

Why did the author give his title as **a servant of God and of the Lord Jesus Christ** instead of calling himself the brother of Jesus (James 1:1)? It seems at first glance that such an address would have given the letter more authority, but James is expressing the same humility Paul used in his letters (Rom. 1:1; Phil. 1:1; Col. 1:23; Titus 1:1). The word translated *servant* is the Greek word for slave. James implied with this one word that God and the Lord Jesus Christ receive his total obedience and loyalty. It indicates the same kind of submission James calls for in chapter 4.

Who were **the twelve tribes scattered among the nations** (James 1:1)? Many scholars think this is a symbolic way of addressing all Christians, both Jews and Gentiles. However, the **twelve tribes scattered among the nations** was an expression used to describe the Jews dispersed around the world. Perhaps James was addressing the Jewish believers who went out from Jerusalem after Pentecost or after the persecution recorded in Acts 8:4.

Greetings (James 1:1) is a unique opening in New Testament letters, but the term was also used in the letter from the church in Jerusalem to the Gentiles (Acts 15:23). The speech by James recorded in Acts 15 and the book of James are also the only Scripture references where Christians are said to have called on

God's name. Although they are translated differently, the Greek phrase is the same in both references (Acts 15:17; James 2:7). These two incidents strengthen the argument for James being the source of both.

Faith and Trials (James 1:2–4)

Consider it pure joy, my brothers, whenever you face trials of many kinds (v. 2). This startling paradox echoes the words of Jesus in the Sermon on the Mount when He said, "Blessed are you when people insult you, persecute you and falsely say all kinds of evil against you because of me" (Matt. 5:11). Why would anyone consider trials a reason to rejoice? **Because you know that the testing of your faith develops perseverance** (James 1:3). The joy is a response to the potential benefit the trials bring, not to the pain they cause.

WORDS FROM WESLEY

James 1:4

But what is the *perfect work* of patience? Is it anything less than the "perfect love of God," constraining us to love every soul of man, "even as Christ loved us?" Is it not the whole of religion, the whole "mind which was also in Christ Jesus?" Is it not "the renewal of our soul in the image of God, after the likeness of Him that created us?" And is not the fruit of this, the constant resignation of ourselves, body and spirit, to God; entirely giving up all we are, all we have, and all we love, as a holy sacrifice, acceptable unto God through the Son of his love? It seems this is "the perfect work of patience," consequent upon the trial of our faith. (WJW, vol. 6, 487)

The Greek word translated *trials* in verse 2 is the same word translated *tempted* in verses 13 and 14. James had only one word to describe external hardships (trials) and internal impulses to sin (temptations). In English we have two words and often think they are unrelated. However, both trials and temptations can test our faith, making it stronger than it would otherwise be. External hardships test the depth of our faith. Persevering faith permeates every area of life and refuses to doubt God. As it endures trials of all kinds, this kind of faith makes us **mature** (prepared to do what God wants us to do) **and complete** (completely capable of carrying out God's will), **not lacking anything** (victorious in the daily struggle to be more like Jesus) (v. 4).

Faith and Prayer (James 1:5–8)

To many people, **wisdom** (v. 5) means deep thinking and impractical ideas. However, to the Jews (and James), wisdom is knowing how to live as God intends for us to live. A person may be prepared to do God's will—even capable of doing it—but **if any of you lacks wisdom**, he or she will neither know what to do nor how to do it (v. 5). That person **should ask God . . . and it will be given to him** or her (v. 5), because God is the source of wisdom (see Prov. 2:6).

WORDS FROM WESLEY
James 1:5

Wisdom—To understand whence and why temptations come, and how they are to be improved. Patience is in every pious man already. Let him exercise this, and ask for wisdom. The sum of wisdom, both in the temptation of poverty and of riches, is described in the ninth and tenth verses; *who giveth to all*—That ask aright; *and upbraideth not*—Either with their past wickedness, or present unworthiness. (ENNT)

Notice how God gives wisdom. He **gives generously to all without finding fault** (James 1:5). He gives more than what is needed and He does it without making anyone feel bad about asking. Consequently, the one who is prepared to do God's will and who is capable of doing it can now know what to do and how to do it.

WORDS FROM WESLEY

James 1:6

But let him ask in faith—A firm confidence in God. St. James also both begins and ends with faith: (ch. 5:15.) The hinderances of which he removes in the middle part of his epistle, *He that doubteth is like a wave of the sea*—Yea, such are all who have not asked and obtained wisdom: *driven with the wind*—From without: *and tossed*—From within, by his own unstableness. (ENNT)

But there is a condition on how a person asks. **When he asks, he must believe and not doubt** (v. 6). The person must be sure of God's power and determination to give. If that person is **double-minded** (v. 8), both trusting and doubting God at the same time, then the person in question **should not think he** or she **will receive anything from the Lord** (v. 7). **He** or she **who doubts is like a wave of the sea, blown and tossed by the wind** (v. 6). That person is unable to determine the direction of his or her life. The lack of faith makes that person **unstable in all he** or she **does** (v. 8). That person will not stand the test of the trials that come along. That person needs to pray, "Help me overcome my unbelief!" (Mark 9:24).

WORDS FROM WESLEY

James 1:8

A double-minded man—Who has, as it were, two souls, whose heart is not simply given up to God: *is unstable*—Being without the true wisdom, perpetually disagrees both with himself and others. (ENNT)

DISCUSSION

While few people look forward to trials, we can still think of them as opportunities for God to make us holy.

1. James mentions trials his readers faced. What kinds of trials might those have been?

2. Define *double-mindedness*.

3. We sometimes question God when we suffer. What was God's response when Job questioned Him (see Job 38:3–7)?

4. According to James, what is the relationship between suffering, faith, perseverance, and maturity?

5. In what specific ways can things like frustration or pain cause us to grow?

6. Has God ever provided wisdom for you? Describe that occasion.

7. How do you react when you boldly ask God for His assistance but the trial doesn't go away? How should you react?

8. If trials are a gift, who should you thank?

9. What are you suffering now and what are you learning from it?

PRAYER

Father, help us remember that You work out everything for our good and for Your purpose: to be conformed to the image of Your Son. Amen.

2

THE GIVER OF PERFECT GIFTS

James 1:9–18

God provides for the personal and spiritual needs of each individual.

The temptation to compare ourselves with one another is both subtle and ever present. Whether we have much or little, it is easy to slip into the habit of gauging ourselves by those around us. On the highway, we may notice what others are driving and wish we had a better vehicle. While browsing in a store, we may take note of what others are wearing and think, "I would never wear that outfit!"

When we make such judgments, we're looking in the wrong direction both for success and for feelings of worth, according to James. This study reminds us that there is only one source for the good things in our lives—our Father in heaven.

COMMENTARY

As noted in the previous study, James wrote to scattered Jewish believers wherever they might be. The Jewish dispersion had been developing since the time of the captivity of the northern kingdom by Assyria about 722 B.C. followed by the captivity of the southern kingdom by Babylon about 586 B.C. The dispersion had increased greatly under the Hellenistic empires founded by Alexander and his successors, and it continued under Roman dominance. Thus, Paul and his associates counted on a Jewish synagogue in many of the towns and cities to which they carried the gospel. Jewish Christian believers apparently followed the same patterns of dispersal as nonbelieving Jews. Many new Jewish believers probably returned home after the birth of the church at

Pentecost recorded in Acts 2. It is quite likely that the church at Rome had been started by such Jewish believers. James was writing to those Jewish believers "scattered among the nations" (1:1). Evidently James believed that the Jewish believers had carried their newfound Christian liberty too far. They were correctly convinced that salvation was by faith, not by works, but they seemed to think this also meant they had little or no responsibility for doing good works. Writing in a style similar to that of the Old Testament Wisdom Literature, James called for a practical Christian life based on faith but manifested by good works. In line with the Old Testament understanding, wisdom for James was wisdom for life, applied and practical wisdom. Using a style similar to Proverbs, James' writing appears to jump from topic to topic and sometimes is a bit hard to follow. But always, his message is very practical, calling for Christian faith to be demonstrated by good works.

True Security (James 1:9–11)

The brother in humble circumstances ought to take pride in his high position (v. 9). Poverty and wealth are repeated themes in James. Here he pointed to the fact that the humble brother has nothing of which he should be ashamed. In fact, as a believer who has been adopted into the family of God, he can be proud of his high position. Adopted by God, one is wealthy indeed. Depending on God is the only true security we can have.

WORDS FROM WESLEY

James 1:9

Let the brother—St. James does not give this appellation to the rich: *of low degree*—Poor and tempted; *rejoice*—The most effectual remedy against double-mindedness; *in that he is exalted*—To be a child of God and an heir of glory. (ENNT)

On the other hand, the person who is rich actually faces insecurity if he or she depends on wealth. Wealth is as fleeting as a wildflower in the scorching heat of the sun. It withers and is soon gone. **In the same way, the rich man will fade away even while he goes about his business** (v. 11). **But the one who is rich should take pride in his low position** (v. 10). What does this mean? The *NIV Study Bible* suggests that James may be referring to trials (see 1:2–4, 10–15). If that is the case, the trial of the humble doesn't take away the person's high position in Christ, and the trial of the rich may bring a person low if the wealth is lost. But the rich person can be proud of this low position (materially) if that person has faith in Christ. Christianity gives one a proper perspective. The poorest person, even the slave, has worth in Christ. Wealth often gives one a sense of false security that can be very dangerous to spiritual well-being.

WORDS FROM WESLEY

James 1:10

O ye that *desire* or *endeavour to be rich*, hear ye the word of the Lord! Why should ye be stricken any more? Will not even experience teach you wisdom? Will ye leap into a pit with your eyes open? Why should you any more "fall into temptation?" It cannot be but temptation will beset you, as long as you are in the body. But though it should beset you on every side, why will you *enter into* it? There is no necessity for this: It is your own voluntary act and deed. Why should you any more plunge yourselves *into a snare*, into the trap Satan has laid for you, that is ready to break your bones in pieces? to crush your soul to death? After fair warning, why should you sink any more into "foolish and hurtful desires?" desires as inconsistent with reason as they are with religion itself; desires that have done you more hurt already than all the treasures upon earth can countervail. (WJW, vol. 7, 11)

In the desert region of Palestine, the wildflower that springs up after the rain and then withers in the scorching heat of the sun would have been a familiar sight. Grass and wildflowers graphically portray the condition of the rich. This analogy also applies to anyone who depends on something other than God. Popular culture argues, and we are continually tempted to think, that material things bring security. But they do not. Only God provides true security. This is the message of James offered to both poor and rich.

Perseverance in Trials (James 1:12)

Blessed is the man who perseveres under trial, because when he has stood the test, he will receive the crown of life (v. 12). Trials are a normal part of life, and James may have been talking about such routine trials that come to everyone. But James may have meant trials for Jewish believers that were a result of their faith in Christ. The kinds of trials aren't specified, and it doesn't matter. What matters is the way we respond to them. The importance of persevering under trial is evident from the fact that this is already the second time (see 1:2–4) James referred to the theme of trials and perseverance within the first chapter of his letter. Perhaps he returned to this theme to assure his readers that the reward for perseverance goes beyond the development of character.

The persevering person will also **receive the crown of life that God has promised to those who love him** (v. 12). The winner of a race was crowned with a wreath. The triumphant king wears a crown of gold and jewels. But God has promised that the faithful Christian will receive a crown of eternal life. This was demonstrated when Jesus was raised from the dead and ascended to the right hand of God. James may have intended this promise to encourage believers he knew were facing imminent persecution and possibly death. But this is also a wonderful promise to all who faithfully endure trials whether they are spiritual, physical, emotional, or otherwise.

The Source of Temptation (James 1:13–15)

When tempted, no one should say, "God is tempting me" (v. 13). People have long struggled with questions related to temptation and the source of temptation. James had no doubt about the source: It comes from within each person. Many years ago comedian Flip Wilson popularized the saying "The Devil made me do it." But he was certainly not the first to lay blame on someone else. Adam blamed Eve. Eve blamed the serpent. We all tend to be ready to pass blame to someone else. James said even Christians may say they are being tempted by God, thinking this is a way to show our piety. There are popular notions among Christians that God tempts us to help us grow strong in our faith. Others even argue that God allows Christians to sin in order to keep them humble. But not according to James! (Paul also said this is a mistaken idea: "Shall we go on sinning so that grace may increase? By no means!" [Rom. 6:1–2]). God does not tempt us. Our temptations come from within ourselves as we allow evil desire to grow and lead us into sin.

WORDS FROM WESLEY
James 1:14

Every man is tempted, when—In the beginning of the temptation, *he is drawn away*, drawn out of God, his strong refuge, *by his own desire*—We are therefore to look for the cause of every sin, in (not out of) ourselves. Even the injections of the devil cannot hurt, before we make them our own. And every one has desires arising from his own constitution, tempers, habits, and way of life; *and enticed*—In the progress of the temptation, catching at the bait; so the original word signifies. (ENNT)

Where does evil desire come from? Adam and Eve did not originally have the problem of a sinful nature with which to contend. Eve allowed legitimate desire to grow into evil desire, and that evil desire led her into sin. We now have a twofold problem:

(1) legitimate desires that can turn into evil desires, and (2) a sinful nature that inclines us to evil desires. We believe we can be cured of the second, but the first remains with us throughout life. Desires are a legitimate part of human nature, but they must be focused on good things. James seems to say that we are not really tempted until we allow our minds to be drawn to evil desire. If we do not use our will to turn away from that evil desire, then sin follows: **But each one is tempted when, by his own evil desire, he is dragged away and enticed. Then, after desire has conceived, it gives birth to sin; and sin, when it is full-grown, gives birth to death** (James 1:14–15). We are expected to be in control of our desires. Interestingly, the Buddhist says salvation is to be rid of all desires. In contrast, the Bible says appetites and desires are good, but they must be kept under control. If desires are not controlled, ultimately they lead to death. As Paul said in Romans 7:24–25, "What a wretched man I am! Who will rescue me from this body of death? Thanks be to God—through Jesus Christ our Lord!" God's grace is offered to aid us through the presence of the Holy Spirit in every believer. We are to pray, "Lead us not into temptation" (Matt. 6:13), not because God is leading us that way, but because He can help us choose paths (thoughts) that will avoid unnecessary temptation.

God's Good Gifts (James 1:16–18)

Don't be deceived, my dear brothers. Every good and perfect gift is from above (vv. 16–17). In verses 13–15, James told us that evil does not come from God. Evil is the perversion of good and arises from our free will. In verses 16–17, he affirmed that all that is good comes from God. God's gifts are all good, and all good is God's gift. Furthermore, God does not change capriciously and suddenly afflict us with evil. Rather, He is **the Father of the heavenly lights** (v. 17), Creator of the stars and other heavenly bodies. **The heavenly lights** certainly shed light, but they may shift and cause shadows as well. But not God! He is all light, all good. God even takes evil (trials and affliction, for instance) and turns it into good for us. "And we know that in all things God works for the good of those who love him, who have been called according to his purpose" (Rom. 8:28). But God does not cause the evil. Evil is the result of misused freedom that He gave to humankind. Freedom was another of His good gifts we have perverted. By misusing freedom, Adam fell, and the result has affected all earthly creation. Now, there is natural evil (caused by the fall) and moral evil, sin (caused by the abuse of human freedom). But God is sovereign over all, including the limited freedom He grants to us humans. He can take the worst kind of evil and somehow turn it into good, as demonstrated by the cross and atonement. As we struggle with bad things that happen to good people, we must trust this fact: God is good! God will somehow—in His own time—turn bad things into good for those who faithfully trust Him.

WORDS FROM WESLEY
James 1:17

No evil, but *every good gift*—Whatever tends to holiness, *and every perfect gift*—Whatever tends to glory, *descendeth from the Father of lights*—The appellation of *Father* is here used with peculiar propriety. It follows, *He begat us.* He is the Father of all light, material or spiritual, in the kingdom of grace and of glory, *with whom is no variableness*—No change in His understanding, *or shadow of turning*—In His will. He infallibly discerns all good and evil, and invariably loves one and hates the other. There is in both the Greek words a metaphor taken from the stars, particularly proper where the Father of lights is mentioned. Both are applicable to any celestial body, which has a daily vicissitude of day and night, and sometimes longer days, sometimes longer nights. In God is nothing of this kind. He is mere light. If there is any such vicissitude, it is in ourselves, not in Him. (ENNT)

For us, the greatest of all good is the fact that we are, or can be, born again. **He chose to give us birth through the word of truth, that we might be a kind of firstfruits of all he created** (James 1:18). The **firstfruits** were the first crops to be harvested in the spring or early summer. They were a promise of the greater harvest yet to come. Christ was the "firstfruits of those who have fallen asleep" (1 Cor. 15:20). Because of His resurrection we have hope that we will be resurrected. James said the early believers were firstfruits demonstrating the promise of salvation to all who would later believe. Salvation is the greatest of the good and perfect gifts God provides us. Our witness to what God has done in our lives may be the firstfruits God will use to lead others to believe and find **birth through the word of truth** (James 1:18).

DISCUSSION

In a world where most people purchase their provisions with money they've earned, it's important to cultivate an attitude of gratitude.

1. What is the relationship between pride and failure, according to James 1:9–18? Between suffering and blessing?

2. What is the true source of blessing? To what sources do people generally look for blessing?

3. James pictures our evil desires as enticing us. Describe what that might look like in a person's life.

4. Who is to blame when we succumb to temptation? Who might we try to blame instead?

5. If wealth is not permanent, why is it so alluring?

6. Where does the temptation to give in to evil come from?

7. Who can we blame when we succumb to that temptation?

8. Name some ways we can shift our focus to God and away from the things He provides.

9. Have you ever asked for something but later realized God had given you a better gift by saying no? Describe that occasion.

PRAYER

Father, help us to bear our trials and temptations with joy so that, if we are faithful, we may receive a crown of life. Amen.

3

DO THE WORD

James 1:19–27

Instruction in the truth must be followed by action.

The annual performance evaluation is a fact of life in many employment settings. Every year, employees are rated on their strengths and weaknesses. Plans are made, goals are set, and great improvements are expected for the coming year. Then what happens? Usually nothing. Most often, the daily routines of running a business take priority over implementing the carefully planned changes. At the end of another year, the results of evaluation are likely to be the same.

That should never happen in your spiritual life, according to James. Pointing out what should be obvious, his words tell us that awareness must be followed by action or else it will have no value. This study will provide a look in the mirror—and perhaps a kick in the pants!

COMMENTARY

The epistle of James was written by James the Just, the brother of Jesus, to first-century Jewish Christians who had been scattered throughout the nations. As a prominent leader of the church in Jerusalem, James had undoubtedly at one point been a pastor to many of his readers. At the time of this letter, however, they had very little contact with the apostles and their teaching, and many had drifted into ungodly patterns of living. James wrote as a Jew to Jews, with an awareness of the importance of adhering to the holy laws of God. The grace of God, he understood, does not exempt a Christian from living a life of obedience. Consequently, the letter is filled with warnings, exhortations, and commands for holy living.

Hearing the Word (James 1:19–21)

James began by calling his readers **dear brothers** (v. 19). This letter was written to a Jewish-Christian audience (1:1–2, 16; 2:1) with whom James felt a strong affinity. He had just told them in 1:18 that they had been given spiritual birth through the activity of the Word of God in their lives. Then he warned them to **take note** (1:19) of what that word within them says.

His first warning is for his readers to **be quick to listen** (v. 19). If the Word of God is going to make any impact on our lives, we must first exhibit a readiness to hear it. Paul declared that "faith comes from hearing the message, and the message is heard through the word of Christ" (Rom. 10:17). The Old Testament Israelites experienced revival when Josiah rediscovered the Word of God and had it read to all the people. The writer of Psalm 119 also expressed a deep passion for hearing the Word that resulted in godly behavior. Christians today must also be eager to listen to what God desires to say to them.

Coupled with the command to listen is the command to be **slow to speak** (James 1:19). A continual talker is unable to hear what anyone else says and is unlikely to hear God as well. Solomon declared, "A man of knowledge uses words with restraint, and a man of understanding is even-tempered. Even a fool is thought wise if he keeps silent, and discerning if he holds his tongue" (Prov. 17:27–28). Some scholars feel the warning here is in regards to speaking publicly on the great doctrines of faith without adequate study. In any event, James warned here and in 3:1–12 that a person's speech often gets him or her in a great deal of trouble and must be closely guarded.

The third command James made in 1:19 is to be **slow to become angry**. Anger closes the mind to God's truth. There is righteous anger that is sometimes appropriate when directed toward sin, but it is usually not the "short fuse" type. A readiness for **anger does not bring about the righteous life that God desires** (v. 20). Proverbs 15:18 says, "A hot-tempered man stirs up dissension." Righteousness does not flourish in an atmosphere of anger. But on the other hand, as James later declares, "Peacemakers who sow in peace raise a harvest of righteousness" (3:18).

James also commanded his readers to **get rid of all moral filth and the evil that is so prevalent** (1:21). God has always required His covenant people to be holy as He is holy. The word for **get rid of** was primarily used in regards to taking off garments (see Heb. 12:1). Thus, a Christian is expected to strip off the prevailing moral filth just as one would a dirty suit of clothes. We do not have to clean up our lives before coming to Christ, but after faith has been born within us, we are expected to let go of sin and live in obedience.

●

WORDS FROM WESLEY

James 1:21

Therefore laying aside—As a dirty garment, *all the filthiness and superfluity of wickedness*—For however specious or necessary it may appear to worldly wisdom, all wickedness is both vile, hateful, contemptible, and really superfluous. Every reasonable end may be effectually answered, without any kind or degree of it. Lay this, every known sin, aside, or all your hearing is vain; *with meekness*— Constant evenness and serenity of mind, *receive*—Into your ears, your heart, your life: *the word*—Of the Gospel; *ingrafted*—In believers, by regeneration (ver. 18), and by habit (Heb. 5:14), *which is able to save your souls*—The hope of salvation nourishes meekness. (ENNT)

James' final command in this section was for his readers to **humbly accept the word planted** in them (James 1:21). Humility is a prerequisite for receiving the Word of God, for God resists the proud. When we acknowledge that we have nothing to stand on except the grace of Christ, then God can bring His Word to life within us. Perhaps James had in mind the parable of the sower and the various kinds of soils in which the seed was planted.

Obeying the Word (James 1:22–25)

James went on to warn his readers: **Do not merely listen to the word** (v. 22). The world is full of people who **merely listen**. This phrase might be used to describe someone auditing a college course, who has no responsibility regarding the classes, but also has no recognition when it comes to graduation. We have not learned until we have put into practice what we have heard. We only **deceive** ourselves if we think that we can gain God's favor through hearing, reading, even memorizing the Word of God without acting on its truths. We must **do what it says** (v. 22). Unless we act on the truth, we show ourselves to be like the foolish man who built his house on the sand (Matt. 7:24–27). This command of James might very well summarize the message of his entire letter.

James illustrated the practice of listening to the Word without putting it into practice by comparing it to **a man who looks at his face in a mirror** (James 1:23). The word for **looks** used here does not refer to a hasty glance, but to careful observation. He studies it until he is thoroughly familiar with its features. He is like the person who intently studies the Word. He is not only familiar with what it says, but he knows exactly what God expects of him.

But **after looking at himself, goes away and immediately forgets what he looks like** (v. 24). The image he sees does not make a very strong impression on his consciousness. The picture

James portrays would seem ridiculous if it weren't so true. How many believers look intently at the Word, but once they walk away from it act as if they had never seen it?

In contrast to the man who looks at the Word and ignores what it has to say, James went on to describe a **man who looks intently into the perfect law** (v. 25) and does exactly what it says. The word for **looks intently** denotes penetrating absorption, like when John stooped and peered into the tomb of Jesus. This man, James says, stoops over the Word of God, zealously searching for its message. He also called it the **perfect law**, revealing both his and his readers' Jewish orientation. But he was not referring to the Old Testament law or the law of Moses, but the law perfected or completed by Jesus. It is also called the **law that gives freedom** (v. 25) because it is not enslaving, like the legalistic code of the Pharisees, but liberating because of the work of the Spirit in the inner man. The one who obeys this law is **blessed in what he does** (v. 25), just like the man described in Psalm 1 who meditates on the law day and night, thereby experiencing God's blessing.

WORDS FROM WESLEY

James 1:25

But he that looketh diligently—Not with a transient glance, but bending down, fixing his eyes, and searching all to the bottom, *into the perfect law*—Of love, as established by faith. St. James here guards us against misunderstanding what St. Paul says concerning the yoke and bondage of the law. He who keeps the law of love is free (John 8:31, &c.), He that does not, is not free, but a slave to sin, and a criminal before God (ch. 2:10), *and continueth therein*—Not like him who forgot it and went away. *This man*—There is a peculiar force in the repetition of the word, *shall be happy*—Not barely in *hearing*, but *doing* the will of God. (ENNT)

Putting the Word into Practice (James 1:26–27)

In James' day, as in our own, it was possible for a person to be **religious** (v. 26) without having that religion affect conduct. The word for **religious** used here describes a person who performs external acts of religion such as public worship, fasting, or giving to the needy. The Jews, to whom James was writing, were steeped in religion where such activity was considered a virtue. Yet it was possible, he asserted, for a person to deceive **himself** into thinking that **religion** has value even if it does not translate itself into godly living (see also v. 22). James said this person's **religion is worthless** (v. 26).

One key area that exposes worthless religion is the area of one's speech. James had more to say about this (see ch. 3), but here he indicated that a person's religion is suspect if he **does not keep a tight rein on his tongue** (1:26). The comparison here is to an unbridled horse that goes wherever it wants. A Christian's speech must be restrained. It is not a virtue to speak one's mind when that speech involves cutting criticism, slander, gossip, uncleanness, or dishonesty. If Christ reigns in our lives, the Spirit will enable us to keep a rein on our speech.

James did not condemn religion in this section. He did, however, attempt to expose hypocritical and empty religious activity. He wanted his religion-minded readers to fully understand the kind of **religion that God our Father accepts as pure and faultless** (v. 27). It is more than liturgy. There is nothing wrong with liturgy—it points the way to the saving work of God. But unless it manifests itself in day-to-day action, it is merely empty words and motion. We must express our love for God in worship, but we must also show our love for God in a tangible way by loving our neighbors.

One act of authentic religion that James singled out is **to look after orphans and widows in their distress** (v. 27). In first-century culture, widows and orphans had little or no means of economic support. If they had no family to care for them, they either starved, begged, or sold themselves as slaves. Ministry to these powerless people had very little "profitable" return for a church, but it demonstrated what genuine service is all about.

In addition to caring for widows and orphans, James said that another demonstration of authentic religion is **to keep oneself from being polluted by the world** (v. 27). From the giving of the law in the Old Testament to the present day, God has been concerned with the holiness of His people. He desires that they be separate from the world's sin (2 Cor. 6:14—7:1). The world is the total system of evil that pervades every sphere of human existence and is set in opposition to God and righteousness. Paul warned the Roman church to avoid being conformed to the world's way of thinking (Rom. 12:2). The apostle John warned his readers as well: "Do not love the world or anything in the world" (1 John 2:15–17). The church in every generation has struggled with identifying specific activities (or attitudes) that might be classified as "worldly." Wesley said that the world is "anything that cools [his] affection for God." His definition still serves us well today.

WORDS FROM WESLEY

James 1:27

The only true *religion* in the sight of God *is this, to visit*—With counsel, comfort, and relief, *the fatherless and widows*—Those who need it most, *in their affliction*—In their most helpless and hopeless state: *and to keep himself unspotted from the world*—From the maxims, tempers, and customs of it. But this cannot be done, till we have given our hearts to God, and love our neighbour as ourselves. (ENNT)

DISCUSSION

A life of authentic holiness is not only about our minds and hearts, but also about how our beliefs translate into actions.

1. How is Scripture like a mirror?

2. What is the relationship between faith and action, according to James?

3. What might happen to a person who hears, but fails to listen and respond, according to Luke 13:25–26?

4. Share a time you found comfort or guidance or even rebuke in the Bible, and it transformed your thinking.

5. Name a trait of a good listener.

6. Do you think the Bible is more like a mirror or a magnifying glass? Why do you think so?

7. What are some ways we might fail to "walk the talk"?

8. Name some practical suggestions for keeping control of our speech.

9. How would you define *purity*? In what practical ways can we keep ourselves pure?

PRAYER

Father, make us doers of the Word and not hearers only. Amen.

THE ROYAL LAW

James 2:1–13

Living as Jesus lived means treating others equally
and not showing favoritism

Selfishness is an insidious habit. It creeps into nearly every area of our lives, causing us to evaluate almost everything in terms of how it might benefit us. And that includes people. Although we were created to love people and use things, we sometimes get those priorities reversed. It is all too easy to begin evaluating others with the question "What can he or she do for me?" in mind.

Giving preference to those who are wealthy, powerful, or beautiful, while ignoring those who seem to have less value, can be a serious problem in the church. The solution, according to James, is love. This study will cause you to take a second look at others—and at yourself—to ensure that you show grace and mercy to all.

COMMENTARY

The general context of this passage is a letter to believers. In it, James taught them that out of their faith in Christ should come the love they have experienced in Christ. Throughout the letter, James gave several examples of how Christ's love is to work. The first (ch. 2) is in regard to showing partiality or discrimination. The second (ch. 3) has to do with ways a Christian's speech might fall short of showing Christ's love. Last he gave examples of worldly behaviors that do not represent Christ, such as arrogance and quarrelsomeness (ch. 4).

Our particular focus comes immediately after James' discourse about putting love into action (1:19–27). James clearly taught that how one lives reflects what one believes, regardless of what the person says or thinks he or she believes. In this section James issued a command—"Don't show favoritism" (2:1)—followed by an example of a wealthy person and a poor person receiving unequal treatment while visiting a meeting place of Christians. After this vivid illustration, James presented two arguments against discrimination. One was a social argument, revealing why discrimination makes no sense socially. Next he offered a moral argument, defining right and wrong and establishing why it is wrong to discriminate. Finally, James reiterated his exhortation and gave a warning against further discrimination.

Likely the people to whom this letter was written were experiencing feelings of displacement and marginalization because they had been "scattered among the nations" (1:1). Common responses accompanying displacement include feelings of insecurity and inferiority. In dealing with these uncomfortable emotions, people make efforts to develop an identity and sense of place within the new setting. Some persons tend to withdraw and look inward, becoming sectarian in their thinking and behavior. Sometimes even self-imposed ghettos are established, with no assimilation into the new setting. It is also not unusual for the marginalized to keep their identities, even becoming proud that they don't belong.

An underlying assumption is that the rich are powerful and are the ones from whom benefit can be derived. Furthermore, it is believed that favor shown to them will be reciprocated. James called for a revolution of social practices. He made it clear that people who are trying to establish their place by discriminating in favor of the rich and against the poor display their lack of love. And, in fact, what they are doing is sinful.

A Clear Command—Do Not Show Favoritism (James 2:1)

James was clear when he issued this command. He used a present tense, imperative (command) form, indicating that he knew the behavior was presently happening, and demanded that it stop immediately. It is not a hypothetical or speculative suggestion: "In case you were wondering if it might be OK, it's not such a great idea to show favoritism." The Greek, in fact, is stronger than the English, **Don't show favoritism**. It says, "You are showing favoritism and (for a believer) it is forbidden. Stop showing favoritism!"

WORDS FROM WESLEY

James 2:1

My brethren—The equality of Christians, intimated by this name, is the ground of the admonition; . . . *the Lord of glory*—Of which glory all who believe in Him partake; *with respect of persons*—That is, honour none, merely for being rich; despise none, merely for being poor. (ENNT)

A Picture Painted—Rich Man and Poor Man (James 2:2–4)

The illustration that follows is hypothetical but vivid. It shows a wealthy man **wearing a gold ring and fine clothes** (v. 2) entering the meeting place of the Christian believers. In contrast, a shabbily attired **poor man** also enters. The wealthy man's ring would seem to indicate not only wealth, but also power and arrogance. His toga is that of a dignitary of the equestrian rank and possibly a candidate for public office. In contrast, the poor person has no ostentatious accessories. The word for his **shabby clothes** identifies his status as a beggar and implies that he is filthy and smelly as well as tattered. The poor man has but mere essentials in a state of disrepair. The picture James painted for his readers is brilliant.

Eager to please and find favor with the distinguished person, the believers welcome and usher him in, leading him to a good seat, a place of honor. We can almost hear each of them wishing, "By me! By me!" The poor man, in contrast, is not guided to a respectable place but merely hurried out of sight so that the "important" person can be preened. The poor man is directed to a lowly place: "You! Sit over there, out of the way!" Actually, **by my feet** (v. 3) means under my footstool. In Mediterranean culture, feet were the least respected parts of the body. To be required to attend to the needs of another's feet was the role of the lowliest slave. We recall that Jesus chose such an act to illustrate His servanthood. This poor man is told to sit at the feet of the believer, implying his inferior status—or perhaps even suggesting that this poor seeker would be responsible to care for the feet of the condescending believer. James essentially said, "This is the picture. You can see yourself here, can't you?"

Social Argument against Discrimination (James 2:5–7)

We must be aware of typical social expectations of this time. Persons of this culture were very aware of their place and it was an honorable thing to keep their place. This would include offering a seat of honor to someone of a higher social rank. However, James said, by maintaining their discriminatory practices, it was impossible to keep a higher law, the law of love. What he suggested was social revolution, "turning the world upside down" (see Acts 17:6).

James lovingly commanded their attention using the address, **My dear brothers** (James 2:5). He encouraged them to look at their own situations; furthermore, he pointed out the way "important people" have typically acted toward **those who are poor in the eyes of the world** (v. 5), that is, his readers. They themselves are being exploited by the powerful. He encouraged them to remember the way the "important" people responded to

Christ—**slandering the noble name of him to whom you belong** (v. 7). He was arguing, "Why would you show honor to those who blaspheme your Lord?" God himself sets the example: He is no respecter of persons (Acts 10:34; Rom. 2:11; Gal. 2:6; 4:28; Eph. 6:9). His association and defense of the poor and downtrodden were the "important" people's primary charge against Him.

James noted that those whom Christ chose were not valued highly in the world's system. He taught that the kingdom has a different value system in that a person who is **rich in faith** (James 2:5) inherits the power of the kingdom of heaven. He indicated that the "important" people of the world treat the poor completely opposite of what God himself does. He honored those who are **poor in the eyes of the world** (v. 5), while the "important" people insulted them.

●

WORDS FROM WESLEY

James 2:5

Hearken—As if he had said, stay, consider, ye that judge thus. Does not the presumption lie rather in favour of the poor man? *Hath not God chosen the poor*—That is, are not they whom God hath chosen, generally speaking, poor *in this world*; who yet are *rich in faith, and heirs of the kingdom*—Consequently the most honourable of men? And those whom God so highly honours, ought not ye to honour likewise? (ENNT)

Moral Argument against Discrimination (James 2:8–11)

James went on to define right versus wrong; that is, he established that the right behavior is to show deference to all, rich and poor alike. He cited the Hebrew Scriptures' **royal law** . . . **"Love your neighbor as yourself"** (v. 8). In verse 9, he stated that to **show favoritism** is not merely a social foible, but **sin.** Contrary to every aspect of God's law, showing favoritism breaks an over-arching tenet governing personal relationships. This law—the law of love—is an expression of God's will. It cannot be toyed with or obeyed only when convenient; it cannot be bypassed when it becomes a hindrance on the social ladder.

James went on to clarify that disagreeing with this law of love is not a minor infraction. It is a serious breach of God's law. God puts it into the same category as two hideous offenses—adultery and murder. James said, **If you do not commit adultery but do commit murder, you have become a lawbreaker** (v. 11). In other words, you are every bit as much convicted by the law as if you had done both.

Final Exhortation and Warning (James 2:12–13)

James concluded by saying, "Now that you understand why discrimination is unjust as well as foolish, be sure to temper your judgments of people with mercy, and you, in turn, will be **judged by the law that gives freedom**" (v. 12). Echoes of the Sermon on the Mount and the words of Paul are heard here (see Matt. 5:7; 7:1–2; Rom. 2:1). **Mercy** (James 2:13), like love (1 Cor. 13:8) will ultimately **triumph over judgment** (James 2:13), so be sure you are on the side of mercy! Be alert to where you could sin—in the area of discrimination. James pointed out that it is logical that those who have experienced mercy instead of judgment would also be sensitive to show mercy, that is, to honor to even the "lowest" of society.

James' message that a believer's faith and actions must be intertwined is reiterated. He insisted that believers show the love of Christ in how they **speak and act** (v. 12). He said that if one speaks as a believer who has received mercy (that is, the person has not been discriminated against by Christ), then certainly the believer is expected to act mercifully toward others regardless of social rank. There is no time in the believer's life when snobbery is appropriate. We are to respect purpose and character but remain unimpressed by status because it will all pass away.

WORDS FROM WESLEY

James 2:12

So speak and act—In all things, *as they that shall be judged*— Without respect of persons, *by the law of liberty*—The Gospel; the law of universal love, which alone is perfect freedom. For their transgressions of this, both in word and deed, the wicked shall be condemned. And according to their works, done in obedience to this, the righteous will be rewarded. (ENNT)

Discrimination reflects an insecurity with our own status, a dissatisfaction with the state in which we find ourselves. Randolph O. Yeager wrote, "The glory of the Lord dazzles the eyes of the true worshiper so much that he is not impressed, for he does not even see the tawdry display of wealth on parade on the one hand or abject poverty on the other. The grace of God is a great leveler." Christ, our supreme example, did not hesitate to give up His place of glory so that we might know His kingdom. When focusing on Him, our social distinctions fade, allowing His love to flow through us. He encourages us with, "Whatever you did for one of the least of these brothers of mine, you did for me" (Matt. 25:40).

DISCUSSION

Preferential treatment is common and accepted, but the way of Christ is to treat the poor and broken with dignity and honor.

1. What example does James give to illustrate favoritism? What might be a current example of favoritism?

2. What is the royal law? Why do you think James would use the word *royal* to describe it?

3. What differences does James indicate between the rich and the poor?

4. In practice, what does it mean to love others as you love yourself?

5. Describe one way we might show prejudice toward those who are rich.

6. What is the relationship between judgment and mercy, according to James?

7. Why do you think Christians are sometimes perceived as judgmental by others? Is that a fair assessment? Why or why not?

8. Describe an occasion when you felt prejudice toward someone else. Describe a time when you felt unfairly judged by others. How did it feel in each case?

9. Do you think it is possible for people who seem to have nothing in common to treat each other with respect? How could they go about doing so?

PRAYER

Father, let us love our neighbors as ourselves no matter their socioeconomic standing, education, or color. Amen.

COMPLETE FAITH

James 2:14–26

Faith must be complemented by action.

Those who watch trends in the church and culture are often troubled by the disconnect between faith and behavior in professing Christians. Surveys routinely reveal that a very high percentage of the population claims to be born again, yet those same surveys reveal that the incidence of immoral behavior continues to rise, while church attendance, Bible reading, and other religious activities decline.

Though trend-watching might not have been as popular in the first century as it is today, James didn't need to conduct a survey to notice that the early Christians seemed quite willing to "talk the talk" without "walking the walk." This study will cause you to examine your life and to close the gap between what you say and what you do.

COMMENTARY

One theme that seems to run through the book of James is the problem of inconsistency in human behavior. This inconsistency is seen in how one treats the rich and the poor, in how one speaks, and in how one does not practice what is heard. James called the inconsistent person "double-minded" (1:8), in contrast to the "perfect" person (3:2), who is consistent in speech and action.

This section on faith and works deals with the same issue: inconsistency. Some would argue that one can have faith, but works are unnecessary. James would have none of that. He argued that the two are inseparable: Faith must demonstrate itself in works of charity just as works of charity are evidence of faith.

The Thesis Stated: Faith without Action Is Dead (James 2:14–17)

James began this section with two simple questions: **What good is it, my brothers, if a man claims to have faith but has no deeds? Can such faith save him?** (v. 14). In the first question the answer is implied: It is not much good. In the second question, however, the Greek grammar clearly indicates an expected negative answer.

●

WORDS FROM WESLEY

James 2:14

From ch. 1 ver. 22 the apostle has been enforcing Christian practice. He now applies to those who neglect this, under the pretence of faith. St. Paul had taught that a man is justified by faith without the works of the law. This some began already to wrest, to their own destruction. Wherefore St. James purposely repeating (ver. 21, 23, 25) the same phrases, testimonies, and examples which St. Paul had used (Rom. 4:5; Heb. 11:17, 31), refutes not the doctrine of St. Paul, but the error of those who abused it. There is therefore no contradiction between the apostles; they both delivered the truth of God; but in a different manner, as having to do with different kinds of men. On another occasion St. James himself pleaded the cause of faith (Acts 15:13, 21). And St. Paul himself strenuously pleads for works, particularly in his latter epistles. (ENNT)

James then gave an example to illustrate his first question: **Suppose a brother or sister is without clothes and daily food. If one of you says to him, "Go, I wish you well; keep warm and well fed," but does nothing about his physical needs, what good is it?** (vv. 15–16). Obviously, the person is still cold and hungry. Such **faith** does no good. It is **dead** (v. 17).

James may have been thinking of a specific example in the church, or he may have simply been using a hypothetical illustration. It is not clear. **Brother or sister** identifies the individual as a Christian **without clothes** (v. 15). In the first-century Roman world, people usually wore two layers of clothing: a short, light undergarment and a larger, thicker cloak. The term translated **without clothes** can literally mean naked (see Mark 14:52), but it can also refer to a person who is not sufficiently clothed. It may refer to one who lacked the more substantial outer garment (see John 21:7). In either case, this brother or sister could be in danger from the elements. This person is also **without . . . daily food** (James 2:15), a term that may indicate the individual does not have food on a regular basis, or that he or she does not have food for that particular day. Thus, James was not necessarily referring to one who was in utter destitution. He may have been referring to those who did not have adequate resources. The words *hungry* and *naked* were often used to refer to those who were disadvantaged (see Matt. 25:31–46).

This example illustrates that for James, *deeds* primarily mean acts of charity. A person who claims to have faith must be willing to use his or her resources to help those in need.

The Thesis Defended (James 2:18–19)

James then responded to a hypothetical situation: **But someone will say, "You have faith; I have deeds." Show me your faith without deeds, and I will show you my faith by what I do** (v. 18). This literary form is known as a *diatribe*. This first-century type of speech was developed by Cynic and Stoic philosophers and was a very common technique in the classroom. Paul and James both made use of the diatribe. The diatribe was characterized by a hypothetical question and a response. Notice that the question is not addressed to James. If that were the case, we would have to read that James has faith and someone else has deeds. James must then demonstrate that he has faith without action, whereas the opponent must demonstrate his faith by his action. That is not the case, however, as James was arguing exactly the opposite point. It was James who would demonstrate that faith requires action. The someone, then, was someone like James. The examples James used, however, were not of himself, but of two completely different characters: Abraham and Rahab.

WORDS FROM WESLEY

James 2:18

But some men will say, with the apostle James, "Show me thy faith without thy work" (if thou canst, but indeed it is impossible); "and I will show thee my faith by my works." And many are induced to think that good works, works of piety and mercy, are of far more consequence than faith itself, and will supply the want of every other qualification for heaven. . . .

And this cannot be denied, our Lord himself hath said, "Ye shall know them by their fruits:" By their works ye know them that believe, and them that believe not. But yet it may be doubted, whether there is not a surer proof of the sincerity of our faith than even our works, that is, our willingly suffering for righteousness' sake: Especially if, after suffering reproach, and pain, and loss of friends and substance, a man gives up life itself; yea, by a shameful and painful death, by giving his body to be burned, rather than he would give up faith and a good conscience by neglecting his known duty. (WJW, vol. 7, 50–51)

Before James gave his human examples, however, he made an analogy to the spirit world. **You believe that there is one God. Good! Even the demons believe that—and shudder** (v. 19). There are several things we need to observe here. First, the NIV translation of this verse makes a statement about monotheism: There is one God and there are no others. This translation, however, does not do justice to the grammar of the passage. A better translation would be "You believe that God is one. Good!" The emphasis is on the character of God. He is single in purpose. This translation also fits best with James' overall theme in which he contrasted the singleness of God with the "double-mindedness" of people.

The expression about the "oneness" of God derives from Deuteronomy 6:4: "Hear, O Israel: The LORD our God, the LORD is one." It is the opening verse of the passage known to Jewish readers as the *shema* (Deut. 6:4–9), a Hebrew word translated as "hear." The *shema* was the central text of the Jewish religion and would have been recited several times each day. It is likely that James' statement, **there is one God** (James 2:19), would have prompted the reader to finish the *shema*: "Love the LORD your God with all your heart and with all your soul and with all your strength" (Deut. 6:5).

Recognition of the oneness of God must result in the love of God and others. Simple belief in the unity of God is inadequate. The demons believe that God, with His single-mindedness, is consistently their enemy. Thus, they shudder. The term **shudder** (James 2:19) was commonly used to denote horror or fear. Interestingly, however, it is also commonly used in what scholars have identified as "magical" papyri (plural of *papyrus*). These papyri contain numerous formulas for exorcisms, the result being that the demons will "shudder."

The Thesis Illustrated: Abraham and Rahab (James 2:20–25)

James then gave two examples of faith: Abraham and Rahab. Again James used the diatribe: **You foolish man** [literally, "empty man"]**, do you want evidence that faith without deeds is useless** [literally, "works-less," a wordplay on "works"]**? Was not our ancestor Abraham considered righteous for what he did when he offered his son Isaac on the altar?** (vv. 20–21; see also Gen. 22:1–14). James drew two slightly different but complementary conclusions from the Genesis account: (1) **You see that his faith and his actions were working together,** (2) **and his faith was made complete by what he did** (James 2:22).

●

WORDS FROM WESLEY

James 2:21

Was not Abraham justified by works?—St. Paul says he was justified by faith, Rom. 4:2, &c. Yet St. James does not contradict him. For he does not speak of the same justification. St. Paul speaks of that which Abraham received many years before Isaac was born, Gen. 15:6. St James of that which he did not receive, till he had offered up Isaac on the altar. He was justified therefore in St. Paul's sense, that is, accounted righteous, by faith antecedent to his works. He was justified in St. James's sense, that is, made righteous, by works subsequent to his faith. So that St. James' justification by works is the fruit of St. Paul's justification by faith. (ENNT)

It was Abraham's actions, James argued, that gave meaning to a text earlier in the Genesis narrative: **"Abraham believed God, and it was credited to him as righteousness"** (v. 23; Gen. 15:6), where Abraham accepted God's promise for many descendants. Abraham's actions thus demonstrated his faith. It was for this reason that **he was called God's friend** (James 2:23). The Genesis narrative does not call Abraham God's friend. James probably had in mind 2 Chronicles 20:7, where Jehoshaphat referred to "Abraham your friend."

The example of Abraham, James argued, proved his thesis: **You see that a person is justified by what he does and not by faith alone** (James 2:24). The term **justified** means to be placed in a proper relationship with God. Unfortunately, English translations do not allow us to see that the verb *to justify* is the same root as the adjective *righteous* and the noun *righteousness*. Thus, one who is justified is righteous.

One is immediately confronted with a quandary. How is it that James said faith without works is dead, and Paul said one is justified by faith, apart from works (see Gal. 2; Rom. 3–4)? This tension is clearly seen when the texts are placed side by side:

You see that a person is justified by what he does and not by faith alone (James 2:24). "For we maintain that a man is justified by faith apart from observing the law" (literally, apart from works of the law; Rom. 3:28).

WORDS FROM WESLEY

James 2:24

Ye see then that a man is justified by works, and not by faith only—St. Paul, on the other hand, declares, a man is justified by faith, and not by works (Rom. 3:28). And yet there is no contradiction between the apostles; because, 1. They do not speak of the same faith; St. Paul, speaking of *living* faith, St. James here of *dead* faith. 2. They do not speak of the same works: St. Paul speaking of works antecedent to faith, St. James of works subsequent to it. (ENNT)

Careful attention to the context will show that the tension is primarily on the surface and the contrast is more apparent than real. First, Paul and James used the term *works* in quite different ways. James used the term primarily to refer to acts of charity such as feeding the hungry, helping widows and orphans, or showing hospitality. The example of Abraham indicates, however, that the term could be understood in a broader sense as responding to a command of God.

Paul used *works* in the phrase "works of the law." Most scholars of Paul understand this phrase as a technical term. It refers to how the Jewish people used the law to identify themselves as a separate people. In the book of 1 Maccabees (a historical book in the Apocrypha), we read about a severe persecution inflicted on the Jewish people by the Syrian ruler Antiochus IV during the second century before Christ. Antiochus outlawed Sabbath observance, destroyed copies of the Torah (the five books of Moses), killed women who had their children circumcised, and forced people to eat pork that had been sacrificed to Greek gods. People who did not follow Antiochus' laws were killed or tortured in extreme ways. Eventually the Jewish people revolted and were free to follow the law again. As a result of the persecution under Antiochus, however, four tenants of the law became preeminent: (1) circumcision, (2) against the eating of swine flesh, (3) Sabbath observance, and (4) against idolatry. These laws in particular gave the Jewish people a sense of identity, becoming boundary markers that separated them from the Gentiles.

In the early church, the question naturally arose, "Do Gentiles have to become Jews to be saved?" In particular, "Do they need to follow the boundary markers?" Many in the early church thought so (see Acts 15:1; Gal. 2:12), but Paul was quite clear in arguing that Gentiles were accepted by God through faith in Christ, not through the "works of the law." The boundary markers that at one time had given the Jewish people a healthy sense of identity had become a source of discrimination against Gentiles, and did not need to be followed.

Thus, Paul was not arguing against good works. On the contrary, he clearly argued that true faith will result in action. Circumcision ("works of the law") is not important. What is important is "faith expressing itself through love" (Gal. 5:6).

Second, both James and Paul appealed to Genesis 15:6, but they do so for different reasons. Paul argued that Abraham was justified by God *before* he had received circumcision (Gen. 17). So Gentile converts do not need to be circumcised or follow the "works of the law." James, on the other hand, appealed to the story of the offering of Isaac (Gen. 22) to show that Abraham's justifying faith resulted in obedience.

James gave one additional example to illustrate his point: **In the same way, was not even Rahab the prostitute considered righteous for what she did when she gave lodging to the spies and sent them off in a different direction?** (James 2:25). The laws of hospitality were primary in the ancient Near East (see, for example, Gen. 18:1–15; Judg. 19). Her hospitality gave further evidence of her faith in God: "For the LORD your God is God in heaven above and on the earth below" (Josh. 2:11).

Conclusion: The Thesis Restated (James 2:26)

James concluded this section by restating his thesis and giving one final analogy: **As the body without the spirit is dead, so faith without deeds is dead** (v. 26). The Greek word *pneuma* can be translated as *spirit* or *breath*. It refers to the life force within a person. Faith without action is a corpse. We see that the contrast is not between faith and works, but between a faith that works and one that does not.

DISCUSSION

Authentic faith is revealed when the words we say are reflected in the way that we live.

1. According to James, what is the relationship between salvation, faith, and action?

2. In what ways does the salvation of Abraham illustrate the relationship between faith and action?

3. In what practical ways does James expect faith to translate into action?

4. Does grace cover our inaction? Why or why not?

5. Do you think most Christians rely most heavily on faith or on action as an evidence of their relationship with God? Explain.

6. What might be the result of relying on grace without taking action?

7. What might be the result of relying on what you do but ignoring grace?

8. List three ways you can have faith, but fail to act on it.

9. Name three ways you could put your faith into action.

PRAYER

Father, may we keep a careful balance of faith and works in all we say and do. Amen.

THE POWER TO BLESS

James 3:1–12

We must use the power of speech to do good rather than harm.

Words have power. Your words have power. You have power. The things you say have the power to build up or tear down others. You can be a force in another person's life, for better or worse, simply by saying words. Most of us don't realize that fact when we are speaking, but we know it well enough when we are listening. We know the things others say to us can make us feel either valuable or worthless.

James strongly challenged Christians to think before they speak and to make their speech a force for good in the world. This study will cause you to examine your patterns of interaction with others and ensure that you are using your power for good.

COMMENTARY

The literary style of James' letter is proverbial. James wrote about practical matters of the Christian faith in something akin to maxims. He gave pithy instruction and exhortation regarding how one is to conduct oneself as a Christian. On at least fifteen different occasions in this short letter, James used the salutation "my brothers," "dear brothers," or simply "brothers" to indicate who he was addressing. James was clearly writing to Christians.

In general, James was encouraged his brothers and sisters in Christ to distinguish themselves from the world with their orientation to life and their basic conduct. In this formative era of the early church, it was important for the believers not simply to know what they believed, but also to know how to behave in this world. The Roman Empire, in which the Christian church was embedded, was thoroughly pagan, but also alluring. Christians could easily be enticed to behave as the pagans did, namely by slavishly obeying their basic instincts. James knew it was possible for Christians to intellectually embrace elements of the gospel, but not enact that gospel. Therefore, James laid out a communal ethos for the Christian church.

In other words, he described the way Christians should behave toward each other and in distinctive contrast to the world. He addressed several behavioral issues: how Christians handle suffering; how Christians should treat people from different socioeconomic classes; how Christians should regard their time and opportunities; and the Christian's responsibility toward the marginalized, that is, the poor and needy.

In 3:1–12, James dealt with one of these practical topics regarding Christian conduct: the appropriate use of the tongue. Let's take a look at his advice.

Teaching: A Hazardous Calling (James 3:1–2)

Verse 1 begins with the terse warning **not many of you should presume to be teachers**. This caution was given in direct response to the problematic, liberal attitude regarding teaching so prevalent in the first-century church. The church in the first century was in its embryonic organizational stage. Therefore it had not completely sorted out how it should function in every circumstance. One undefined circumstance was how teachers should be selected. In the vacuum created by an undefined selection process, many Christians not gifted in the transmission of the truth or lazy in their responsibility of teaching took up the task of teaching. James reminded these interlopers that they should not engage in teaching just because it is an attractive profession entailing a modicum of respect. Why? **Because** we **know that**

we who teach will be judged more strictly (v. 1). While it is true that a certain amount of prestige is attributed to teachers, James pointed out the downside to teaching, namely that the teacher will be held accountable for the ideas he or she conveys and the lives he or she shapes—a sober reminder for the prospective teacher.

Verse 2 seems to continue the previous line of thinking by saying **we all stumble in many ways.** This verse infers the proneness of Christians to make mistakes as part of their humanity. As Christians, however, we are held to a higher degree of accountability. Therefore, James reasoned, because the odds of making mistakes are even higher for teachers, so is their level of accountability as Christian teachers. In other words, Christian teachers had better be convinced of their call to teach and compelled by their giftedness.

●

WORDS FROM WESLEY

James 3:2

The same is able to bridle the whole body—That is, the whole man. And doubtless some are able to do this, and so are in this sense perfect. (ENNT)

In verse 2, James also expanded the discussion beyond the issue of the hazards of teaching when he said **if anyone.** From this point on he no longer talked about teachers alone, but all Christians. **Is never at fault in what he says** (v. 2) indicates that James narrowed his presentation to spoken words. It is the Christian's speech, therefore, that James addressed. This person, whose words are faultless, **is a perfect man, able to keep his whole body in check** (v. 2). This statement foreshadows the points James was about to make. It is something of a pre-summary of what is about to be said. James clearly believed that speech is the most difficult aspect of one's life to discipline, but if it can be disciplined, any part of a person's life can be disciplined.

The Tongue: Four Powerful Images (James 3:3–8)

Verse 3 contains the first image: **When we put bits into the mouths of horses to make them obey us, we can turn the whole animal.** In this first image, James enabled us to see the value of a controlled tongue by comparing the controlled tongue to a bit in a horse's mouth. Because the reins of the bridle are connected to the bit, the horseman has control over the horse's movements. The horse is a large beast capable of unpredictable behavior, but with the bit in its mouth, the animal must obey whoever controls the reins. The bit may be small, but it overcomes the strength of the beast, making possible the positive contributions desired by the horse's owner. The horse may provide transportation or engage in strenuous labor, but only if it has a bit in its mouth. The human being is also capable of encouragement and imparting helpful truth, but only if the tongue is controlled. Though small in size, the disciplined tongue can do much good, as indicated in Isaiah 50:4: "The Sovereign LORD has given me an instructed tongue, to know the word that sustains the weary."

James 3:4 provides the second image of the tongue: **Or take ships as an example. Although they are so large and are driven by strong winds, they are steered by a very small rudder wherever the pilot wants to go.** This image, along with the first, demonstrates the potential of the tongue for good. Ships are, of course, large, heavy objects and potentially very difficult to guide. However, if the ship has a rudder (the small, flat, movable device connected to the rear of the ship), the captain can steer the ship wherever he or she wants because he or she controls the rudder from the helm. Although strong winds are trying to force the ship away from the intended direction, as long as the captain controls it, the rudder decides where the ship will go. The analogy is clear: Just as a ship controlled by a small rudder is able to do good things, such as carrying cargo to a destination or providing travelers with a dependable conveyance, so also is the controlled tongue able to do good things.

Verse 5 introduces the third image of the tongue in this passage. The first two images demonstrate the tongue's potential for good. The third and fourth images illustrate the tongue's potential for evil. **Consider what a great forest is set on fire by a small spark. The tongue is also a fire** (vv. 5–6). Once again in James' analogy, the thing likened to the tongue is small and insignificant, in this case, a small spark. A spark may seem benign and inconsequential, but in the wrong place a spark can ignite a blaze that is tremendously destructive. The tongue, although small, has destructive capability as well. Cutting, harsh words or a piece of juicy gossip shared in a sinister manner can have ominous consequences. James seemed to be suggesting that Christians often underestimate the power of words. But he reminded us of their nuclear potential. **It corrupts the whole person, sets the whole course of his life on fire, and is itself set on fire by hell** (v. 6). The potential fire set by the tongue is not just any old fire. It is a fire with massive destructive power. James used words that are translated **the whole person** and **the whole course of his life** to illustrate that with some misspoken words a person's entire life can be destroyed. Such is the power of words.

Verses 7–8 again illustrate the destructive potential of the tongue through a fourth image. This illustration of the tongue reveals it to be wild and unpredictable. **All kinds of animals, birds, reptiles and creatures of the sea are being tamed and have been tamed by man, but no man can tame the tongue.** In these verses, James' writing takes us to the circus. We are to notice that many wild animals have been tamed and are able to perform stunts that amuse us. But the tongue, on the other hand, is impossible to tame. James engaged in a little hyperbole by saying the tongue is unable to be tamed; however, it is able to be tamed when submitted to the will of the Holy Spirit. He emphasized that it is untamable to make us aware of just how unruly it tends to be. Even more unruly than a ferocious lion, a stampeding elephant, or a deadly rattlesnake, verse 8 calls the tongue **a restless evil**. As a predatory animal is always lurking for unsuspecting prey, so the tongue is lurking as well and apt to cause just as much trouble.

WORDS FROM WESLEY
James 3:8

But no man can tame the tongue—Of another: no, nor his own, without peculiar help from God. (ENNT)

An Exhortation to Be Vigilant and Holy in Our Speech (James 3:9–12)

Verse 9 begins James' summation of the matter of the tongue. In this summation, the author took on the role of an exhorter. He reminded readers of what he said and then encouraged them to be consistent in their speech. **With the tongue we praise our Lord and Father, and with it we curse men, who have been made in God's likeness.** James evidently saw inconsistency among Christians in the matter of speech. He pointed out that you cannot be truly Christian in praising God if at other times you slanderously speak about others. This behavioral dichotomy is evidence of double-mindedness in the Christian—a subject James addressed in 1:6–8. James also pointed out in 3:9 that to curse people is really cursing God, since we are made in God's image. Verse 10 says, **Out of the same mouth come praise and**

cursing. My brothers, this should not be. Here the passage reaches a crescendo. James pleaded with his fellow Christians to be careful in speech. He urged them not to let their passions rule them, evidenced by departing from righteous and appropriate speech.

WORDS FROM WESLEY
James 3:9

Men made after the likeness of God—Indeed we have now lost this likeness. Yet there remains from thence an indelible nobleness, which we ought to reverence both in ourselves and others. (ENNT)

Verse 12 says, **My brothers, can a fig tree bear olives, or a grapevine bear figs?** Here James alluded to a famous statement of Jesus made in the Sermon on the Mount (Matt. 7:16–20). The point is, just as a fig tree doesn't bear olives or a grapevine bear figs, a child of God doesn't produce incessant indiscretions of the tongue.

DISCUSSION

Our words can inadvertently confirm a person's lack of self-worth; better to use them to help a person find hope and healing in Christ.

1. Why will teachers and leaders be judged more strictly? Is that fair? Why or why not?

2. Describe the power of words and give some examples.

3. What point is James making in the example of fresh water versus salt water (see James 3:11)?

4. In what ways can careless speech play into the scheme of the Enemy to steal, kill, and destroy?

5. Share a story from Scripture where Jesus rebuked careless words.

6. Define *gossip*.

7. Explain why you agree or disagree with the saying: "Sticks and stones may break my bones, but words will never hurt me."

8. Lying is one way to get in trouble with words. What are some others?

9. Why is it so difficult for us to control the words we say?

10. List some practical ways you can use words to do good rather than harm.

PRAYER

Father, "May the words of [our mouths] and the meditation of [our hearts] be pleasing in your sight" (Ps. 19:14). Amen.

TWO WAYS OF THINKING

James 3:13–18

We live by heavenly wisdom, not the wisdom of the world.

All of us make decisions every day. Some of them are of little consequence, but others may have serious implications for the future. How do you know if you're making right choices? What evidence can you point to that says you're on the right track? Is there a magic formula for gauging the wisdom of any course of action?

God freely gives wisdom, according to James, and it is easily apparent when we are following the wisdom of God or the desires of our own hearts—that will soon be revealed by the quality of our lives. This study will help you evaluate the sources of input that are shaping your life choices and become more firmly dependent on the wisdom that comes from God.

COMMENTARY

The book of James is often thought of as a collection of practical advice about how to live the Christian life. Some would argue that there is not much connection between its various sections. However, James 3:13–18 has close affinities with what goes before and what comes after. The first twelve verses of chapter 3 talk about our inability to control our tongues, our speech. Because of what is in our hearts, it seems like we cannot control our tongues. They will speak what is harmful as well as what is good. Verses 13–18 show that the true wisdom from above is the answer to this uncontrolled tongue and the dissension and destruction it brings.

Although the word *wisdom* is not used in James 4:1–10, these verses further describe the destructive influence that comes from false, worldly wisdom. They then tell us how to appropriate the wisdom that is from God (vv. 7–10) in our lives, followed by a warning against speaking evil (vv. 11–12). This warning reminds us of James' discussion of the tongue in 3:1–12. The "good life" of 3:13 is the same as the washed hands and purified heart of 4:8.

Indeed, if James is giving us a collection of teachings on practical Christian living, then James 3:13–18 could be seen as its heart. For all practical Christian living is based on the true wisdom from heaven described in these verses. The heart that is filled with this wisdom is the only heart that can carry out James' instructions. It is the Holy Spirit who implants this wisdom in our hearts.

Are You Wise? (James 3:13)

The question at the beginning of this verse gets our attention and introduces a new topic—true **wisdom**. We are reminded of Proverbs 9:4–5, where wisdom is pictured as a woman: "'Let all who are simple come in here!' she says to those who lack judgment. 'Come, eat my food.'" She calls the simple to teach them true wisdom. James' purpose is similar, although he called out to those **wise and understanding** (James 3:13). He may have really meant, "Those of you who believe you are wise and understanding." He wanted to make sure they had true wisdom.

Wise and *understanding* are terms often used together in relation to true wisdom. James was building on the teaching of the Old Testament. *Wisdom* means neither cunning nor academic ability. It means the ability to live life properly. And, as Proverbs 1:7 makes clear, it begins with "the fear of the LORD." To "fear" God in this sense is to live in accord with the fact that He is our loving Creator and Redeemer. He has put us in His world and we are responsible to Him. Evidently James' readers were tempted to follow a "false" wisdom. What kind of wisdom do we follow?

True wisdom will be shown by a **good life** (James 3:13). These words describe conduct that truly exemplifies Christian character. They indicate a lifestyle that will attract others to Christ by its purity and love. It will be characterized by actions done in **humility** or meekness. This humility bears with wrongs and does not push oneself ahead of others. It is characterized by honoring others above ourselves (see Rom. 12:10). Such humility or meekness was considered weakness in the pagan world where James' readers lived. Many today consider it weakness. They believe we must be self-assertive, standing up for our own rights. But Christians are not meek because they are weak, rather because they trust God and love others. This humility is the mark of the true wisdom that comes from God.

WORDS FROM WESLEY

James 3:13

Let him show his wisdom, as well as his faith, *by his works;* not by words only. (ENNT)

Human "Common Sense": Wisdom from Below (James 3:14–16)

What are the marks of false wisdom? **Bitter envy and selfish ambition** (v. 14). These English words express the meaning of this text well. **Bitter** refers to a harsh envy that resents wrongs and holds grudges. **Selfish ambition** makes us think of rivalry among groups, us versus them. This kind of ambition foments divisions in order to attain its selfish ends. How many times do divisions within our churches come from principle or from selfish ambition? Selfish ambition may just mean one doesn't want to lose one's position or influence. It could mean that we who have stood by the work and been dependable don't want to lose control of things. Selfish ambition is a matter of power.

If we have **bitter envy and selfish ambition** in our lives and then **boast** about our Christianity, we are denying **the truth** of the gospel (v. 14). We are claiming to be something we are not and are bringing shame on the truth of the gospel. Our lives say to the world that the gospel produces selfish ambition, when the very opposite is true.

Now, the kind of wisdom that puts our own interests first is the "common sense" of human beings. But where does it come from, this kind of **"wisdom"** (v. 15) that leads to selfish ambition? Verses 15 is plain—it **does not come down from heaven** ("from above," KJV). That is, its source is not God. Rather, it **is earthly, unspiritual, of the devil. Earthly** means it pertains only to this world, only to the values of sinful human society. It also is unspiritual, in accord with human nature under the bondage of sin. This selfish wisdom is exactly the way humanity under bondage to sin thinks people should live. The NASB translates **unspiritual** as "natural." This translation is acceptable if we remember that humans are, since the fall, naturally under sin. But this wisdom did not originate in humanity's "common sense." It is ultimately from the Devil. It is from the pit of hell. It comes from the world, the flesh, and the devil. When we follow this wisdom, we are doing what the Devil wants, not what God wants.

Verse 16 gives us the results of **envy and selfish ambition** (the same words as in v. 14)—**disorder and every evil practice**. This is a very broad description and involves confusion and all sorts of vile or base practices. When **envy and selfish ambition** rule, we may do things we never dreamed of doing. James was describing the opposite of the peace, harmony, and wholeness brought by God's wisdom.

WORDS FROM WESLEY

James 3:15

This wisdom which is consistent with *such* zeal: *is earthly*— Not heavenly, not from the Father of lights; *animal*—Not spiritual; not from the Spirit of God: *devilish*—Not the gift of Christ, but such as Satan breathes into the soul. (ENNT)

Divine "Common Sense": Wisdom from Above (James 3:17–18)

After giving us the ugly picture of sinful wisdom based on human common sense, James used seven words and phrases to describe the beauty of true **wisdom** (v. 17). True wisdom **comes from heaven**, that is, from God. He is its author and the one who gives it to us. Rather than being characterized by envy (vv. 14, 16), true wisdom is **pure** (v. 17). Since this wisdom comes from a heart clean of wrongdoing and selfish motive, it does not lead to selfish ambition. Christ's will has taken the place of self-will. Thus, such a heart is **peace-loving**. It wants the best for others and wants to get along with them. Thus, it is **considerate** of the needs of others. It is not servile or gullible but **submissive** to the needs of others rather than putting its own needs first. The KJV translates **submissive** as "easy to be intreated": it is ready to listen to the other person's point of view. Those who live according to this wisdom know that God has mercifully forgiven and accepted them. Therefore they are **full of mercy** toward others. They are ready to forgive and make allowance for others. Demonic "wisdom" led to "every evil practice" (v. 16). This wisdom is full of **good fruit** (v. 17)—every kind of good.

The NIV translates the next quality in verse 17 as **impartial** and the KJV as "without partiality." Certainly James taught us elsewhere that we should show God's love to all (2:1–13). But the translation of the NASB is also possible—"unwavering." This kind of wisdom is not "double-minded" (4:8). It does not waver between God's wisdom and the Devil's wisdom.

Finally, the wisdom from God is **sincere** (3:17; "without hypocrisy," KJV). It is not two-faced. It does not cover a hidden motive or agenda. The person living according to this wisdom is not putting on a show of love to gain selfish ends.

WORDS FROM WESLEY

James 3:17

But the wisdom from above, is first pure—From all that is earthly, natural, devlish: *then peaceable*—True peace attending purity, it is quiet, inoffensive: *gentle*—Soft, mild, yielding, not rigid; *easy to be entreated*—To be persuded or convinced, not stubborn, sour, or morose; *full of good fruits*—Both in the heart and in the life, two of which are immediately specified: *without partiality*— Loving all, without respect of persons: embracing all good things, rejecting all evil; *and without dissimulation*—Frank, open. (ENNT)

Verse 18 depicts the results of the wisdom from above. The result of false wisdom is "disorder" (v. 16), confusion, and all kinds of evil. The result of God's wisdom is peace—not merely peace in the sense of the absence of hostility, but peace as a positive good: wholeness, harmony, love. This life of God's wisdom, of harmony and wholeness, is the **harvest of righteousness** (v. 18). It is the kind of life that results from living in right relationship with God. Those who live according to God's wisdom are **peacemakers** in the deepest sense. Since they are not torn by selfish ambition, their whole lives can be described as sowing **in peace.** James was not saying that they are arbitrators between people who are hostile to one another. They are not just trying to settle people's selfish claims on the basis of mutual self-interest. They are living according to a higher principle—genuine love for those around them.

The question of verse 13 still confronts us: Who of us are wise and understanding? Are we practicing God's true wisdom? Are we living according to human or divine "common sense"? No question is more important. God's grace is adequate to enable us to live according to His wisdom. We must repent of our sins and submit and draw near to Him (4:6–10). We must let Him do a deep work of cleansing in our lives. It is the Holy Spirit who applies the work of Christ to our hearts and enables us to live according to true wisdom.

DISCUSSION

The wisdom of God will help us make decisions that will reflect our love for God and our neighbors.

1. How does James define *wisdom*?

2. Describe the false sort of wisdom James mentions.

3. What is the difference between wisdom and knowledge? Between wisdom and discernment?

4. Would you say wisdom is valued in our culture? Why do you think as you do?

5. What is the relationship between envy and wisdom? Describe how that might work in a practical example.

6. In what ways can we seek wisdom? What sources of advice that are routinely used in our culture do not usually yield wisdom?

7. Based on the list of attributes for wisdom James mentions, do you consider yourself wise? Do you think others would?

8. List several reasons it is important to seek godly counsel.

9. What is one personal goal you have made to grow as a believer?

PRAYER

Father, give us wisdom that comes from above so that we may love those here below. Amen.

A GENUINE HEART CHANGE

James 4:1–10

Repentance produces change.

Who gets the credit for the good things we do? Most of us have no trouble answering that question. We get the credit, of course! Yet we are often eager to share the responsibility for the things we do wrong. Our circumstances conspire against us. Other people put pressure on us. We're tired. We're under stress. When we don't behave well, we often think it's not really our fault.

That's nonsense, according to James. You alone are responsible for your choices and actions. Your evil desires spring from selfishness within you, but there is a remedy. This study will challenge you to take responsibility for your actions and empower you to resist the temptations you face.

COMMENTARY

The book of James has been compared to a string of beads because it seems to have little or no connection between the various topics. Its structure reflects the Jewish sermon pattern of that time. The rabbis taught their students to move quickly from one subject to another in order to keep people listening. James certainly followed that instruction as he moved repeatedly from a principle of how to live a godly life to a call to put God's Word into practice.

The focus on practical Christian living throughout this New Testament book is like the Old Testament Wisdom Literature. If you read through the book of Proverbs, you'll find Solomon making a change in topic as often as every verse. However, the whole point of both Proverbs and James is to instruct God's people about living in a way that pleases the Father.

Like a string of beads with a limited number of colors, James returned to the same topic more than once in his sermon. In James 1:13–15, he pointed out that our desires give rise to temptation, sin, and death. And in James 3:13–18, he called attention to the fact that selfish ambition and envy produce conflict in our relationships with other Christians. He came back to the destructive nature of our fallen desires in chapter 4 as well.

James tied prayer into this discussion of our desires here in chapter 4. He mentioned that a double-minded person's prayers would not be answered (1:2–8). He ended his sermon with the assurance that the prayer of faith is powerful and effective (5:13–18). In this central teaching on prayer, James pointed out the keys to receiving answers to our prayers.

James 4 can be summed up as a call to submit to God. Nearly every area of life is addressed—interpersonal relationships, desires, relationship to God, attitudes, plans, and more. The chapter is centered on James' call to repentance (vv. 8–10).

Broken Relationships (James 4:1–3)

James opened this chapter with a piercing question: **What causes fights and quarrels among you?** (v. 1). **Fights** can range from an atmosphere of discord and strife to outright feuds. **Quarrels** are obvious conflicts and battles.

Why are these things going on in the church? **Don't they come from your desires that battle within you?** (v. 1). In James 1:13–15, the author pointed out that our desires give rise to temptation, sin, and death. This principle echoes the words of Jesus, who said, "Don't you see that nothing that enters a man from the outside can make him 'unclean'? For it doesn't go into his heart but into his stomach, and then out of his body . . . What comes out of a man is what makes him 'unclean.' For from within, out of men's hearts, come evil thoughts, sexual immorality, theft, murder, adultery, greed, malice, deceit, lewdness, envy, slander, arrogance and folly. All these evils come from inside and make a man 'unclean'" (Mark 7:18–23).

This whole problem grows out of our selfish ambitions and envy (James 3:13–18). The process begins when a Christian gives in to the desire for comfort or pleasure. That desire will not be satisfied. The individual may experience some temporary comfort or pleasure, but either the desire will increase until it cannot be satisfied or the source of satisfaction will disappear. That's why **you want something but don't get it** (4:2). When our desires aren't fulfilled, we become frustrated and begin to find someone or someway to find satisfaction. That's when we start to quarrel and fight because nothing and no one can satisfy these desires.

WORDS FROM WESLEY

James 4:2

If it be possible for any direction to be more clear, it is that which God hath given us by the apostle, with regard to prayer of every kind, public or private, and the blessing annexed thereto: "If any of you lack wisdom, let him ask of God, that giveth to all men liberally" (if they ask; otherwise "ye have not, because ye ask not," James 4:2), "and upbraideth not; and it shall be given him" (James 1:5). (WJW, vol. 5, 192)

The root of the problem is that we've not only entertained the wrong desires, but we've also sought fulfillment in the wrong sources. James pointed out that we should be seeking wisdom from God (James 1:2–5; 3:13–18). That will always lead us to prayer. But we **do not have, because** we **do not ask God** (4:2). Our desires are out of control because we need wisdom; we don't have wisdom because we have not asked for it. Even **when** we do **ask** for something in prayer, we **do not receive, because** we **ask with wrong motives**. We pray in order **that** we **may spend what** we **get on** our **pleasures** (v. 3). Our focus in life is on ourselves. We are breaking the great commandments.

Spiritual Adultery (James 4:4–6)

When we don't love God with all our heart, strength, and mind, we are committing "spiritual adultery." This sin was obvious in the Old Testament. Whenever God's people began worshiping idols, the prophets called them to repent of adultery. As Christians, we don't need to bow to a statue in order to sin like the Israelites did. If we give our desires a higher priority in our lives than we give God, we are **adulterous people** (v. 4). If we even begin to think that what we want is on the same level as God's will, we are adulterous people.

So, James said, **You adulterous people, don't you know that friendship with the world is hatred toward God? Anyone who chooses to be a friend of the world becomes an enemy of God** (v. 4). The apostle John said the same thing: "Do not love the world or anything in the world. If anyone loves the world, the love of the Father is not in him. For everything in the world—the cravings of sinful man, the lust of his eyes and the boasting of what he has and does—comes not from the Father but from the world. The world and its desires pass away, but the man who does the will of God lives forever" (1 John 2:15–17). Jesus said, "No one can serve two masters" (Matt. 6:24). We cannot live to serve God while trying to satisfy all our desires at the same time.

We must realize **that the spirit he caused to live in us envies intensely** (James 4:5). This verse can be difficult to understand. Since the earliest manuscripts had no uppercase letters, we cannot know for certain if the **spirit** is the Holy Spirit who dwells in Christians or the human spirit. Since no one Scripture verse records these words, we can't refer to another passage for help in choosing an interpretation. If it is the Holy Spirit, then what does He envy intensely? In the context of this passage and the whole Old Testament, the Holy Spirit would be longing for our complete and undivided love. On the other hand, if James was referring to the human spirit, it always envies intensely because our fallen nature thinks we ought to have more than we will ever receive.

WORDS FROM WESLEY

James 4:4

Consider, what it is which the apostle here means by *the world*. He does not here refer to this outward frame of things, termed in Scripture, heaven and earth; but to the inhabitants of the earth, the children of men, or, at least, the greater part of them. But what part? This is fully determined both by our Lord himself, and by His beloved disciple. First, by our Lord himself. His words are, "If the world hate you, ye know that it hated me before it hated you. If ye were of the world, the world would love its own: But because ye are not of the world, but I have chosen you out of the world, therefore the world hateth you. If they have persecuted me, they will also persecute you. And all these things will they do unto you, because they know not him that sent me" (John 15:18, &c). You see here "*the world*" is placed on one side, and *those who "are not of the world"* on the other. They whom God has "chosen out of the world," namely, by "sanctification of the Spirit, and belief of the truth," are set in direct opposition to those whom He hath not so chosen. (WJW, vol. 6, 454)

In either case, we need God's help to conquer our selfish desires. James held out the promise of that help in his quote from Proverbs 3:34: **"God opposes the proud but gives grace to the humble"** (James 4:6). God **gives us more grace** (v. 6)—more than enough power to overcome this destructive sin.

Submit to God (James 4:7–10)

James offered several solutions in these four verses. He demanded that we give this problem our immediate attention. We dare not wait for a better day to gain the victory over our desires.

First, **submit yourselves, then, to God** (v. 7). Surrender your ambitions and desires to Him. Obey God even if doing so makes you uncomfortable and insecure.

Second, **resist the devil, and he will flee from you** (v. 7). Don't give in to his deceptions. Refuse to listen to him. Put on the spiritual armor God has supplied and pray (Eph. 6:11–18). You will overcome.

Third, **come near to God and he will come near to you** (James 4:8). He will not find fault with you. He is faithful and just to forgive us when we confess our sins.

●

WORDS FROM WESLEY

James 4:8

Then draw nigh to God in prayer, *and he will draw nigh unto you,* will hear you: which that nothing may hinder, *cleanse your hands—* Cease from doing evil, *and purify your hearts—* From all spiritual adultery. Be no more double-minded, vainly endeavouring to serve both God and mammon. (ENNT)

Fourth, **wash your hands, you sinners** (v. 8). "Who may ascend the hill of the LORD? Who may stand in his holy place? He who has clean hands and a pure heart, who does not lift up his soul to an idol or swear by what is false" (Ps. 24:3–4). Stop putting your desires on the same level as God's will.

Fifth, **purify your hearts, you double-minded** (James 4:8). Focus on God and God alone. Stop wavering and commit your entire life to Him. Don't settle for anything less than knowing God and living His way.

Sixth, **grieve, mourn and wail** (v. 9). Express the godly sorrow of true repentance. Grieve over your sins. Mourn for the blessings you've missed because of your prayerlessness. Wail because you've been seeking security and comfort in all the wrong places.

Seventh, **change your laughter to mourning and your joy to gloom** (v. 9). Stop enjoying the satisfaction of your selfish desires. Stop laughing at the misery of those you've attacked. Start mourning over the results of your sins.

Finally, **humble yourselves before the Lord, and he will lift you up** (v. 10). Follow Jesus' example of serving others and waiting for God to honor you (Phil. 2:1–11). Remember Jesus said, "Whoever wants to become great among you must be your servant, and whoever wants to be first must be your slave—just as the Son of Man did not come to be served, but to serve, and to give his life as a ransom for many" (Matt. 20:26–28).

DISCUSSION

When God transforms our hearts, He makes it possible for us to break free from the worldly "wisdom" that has held us captive.

1. Describe the relationship between temptation and disharmony in relationships.

2. What do you think James meant by "friendship" with the world?

3. How would you define *submission* as used in James 4:1–10?

4. Why do you think James would compare wanting your own way to cheating on God?

5. Do you think God really expects perfection? Why or why not?

6. Can you name one instance where it's appropriate to get angry?

7. James said the Devil will flee if resisted. In what specific ways can we resist the Devil?

8. Why do we tend to justify our words and actions, even when we know they are wrong?

9. In what ways might your life need to be purified? How can you seek that type of cleansing?

PRAYER

Father, give us grace to live together in Your love and peace. Amen.

A WISER WAY TO LIVE

James 4:11–17

We are wise to reserve judgment on others and the future.

Most of us have some idea of what the future will hold for us—or at least what we would *like* it to hold. We generally form some plan for each day, write next week's appointments on a calendar, and make our vacation reservations well in advance. Planning makes us effective and productive.

The danger in making such plans is that we may become so focused on our desires for the future that we forget who is really in control of our lives. None of us can control the future, so our plans are really more like hopes. Or as James might put it, they are requests we make to God. This study will force you to look beyond yourself and recognize your dependence on God in practical ways.

COMMENTARY

The fourth chapter of James can be condensed into a plea for Christians to yield their lives to God. Nearly every area of life is tackled—interpersonal relationships, desires, relationship to God, attitudes, plans, and more. The chapter rests on James' appeal for repentance in the preceding verses, 8–10.

The book of James offers few or no ties between the numerous topics presented. Although he didn't stay long on any one topic, James came back to the same subjects more than once in his sermon. He had a great deal to say about the tongue. He said anyone who cannot control his or her tongue is not truly religious (1:26). And in chapter 3, James warned us about the destructive power of the tongue (3:1–12). In this section of chapter 4, he tied controlling the tongue in our relationships to our submission to God. Then James closed the chapter by pointing out that the way we state our plans for the future will reveal the reality or the emptiness of our surrender to God's will.

Don't Judge Each Other (James 4:11–12)

When Christian **brothers** and sisters submit to God, they should **not slander one another** (v. 11). This is the main expression of the fights and quarrels James condemned at the beginning of this chapter. It is also a means of killing another person, according to Jesus (see Matt. 5:21–22).

WORDS FROM WESLEY

James 4:11

Speak not evil one of another—This is a grand hinderance of peace. O who is sufficiently aware of it! He that speaketh evil of another, does in effect speak evil of the law, which so strongly prohibits it. *Thou art not a doer of the law, but a judge*—Of it, thou settest thyself above, and as it were condemnest it. (ENNT)

Anyone who speaks against his brother or judges him speaks against the law and judges it (James 4:11). An attack on another person's character reveals a serious breakdown in our moral judgment. When a Christian chooses to ignore the royal law of love, he or she becomes a lawbreaker (2:8–9). Resorting to slander means that he acts as if he is above God's law. Instead of speaking and acting like one who will be judged by the law (2:12), she conducts herself as though she can judge the law. That person is behaving as though he or she can decide what is right and what is wrong. In other words, **when you judge the**

law, you are not keeping it, but sitting in judgment on it (4:11). You are not submitting to God.

In this passage, the attitude of the person sitting in judgment is the ultimate problem. **There is only one Lawgiver and Judge** (v. 12), and He is the only One who can decide what is right and wrong. If a person attempts to take God's place, then serious judgment will follow. God is **the one who is able to save and destroy** (v. 12). Jesus told His disciples not to fear those who can only kill the body but to fear the One who can destroy both the body and the soul in hell (Matt. 10:28).

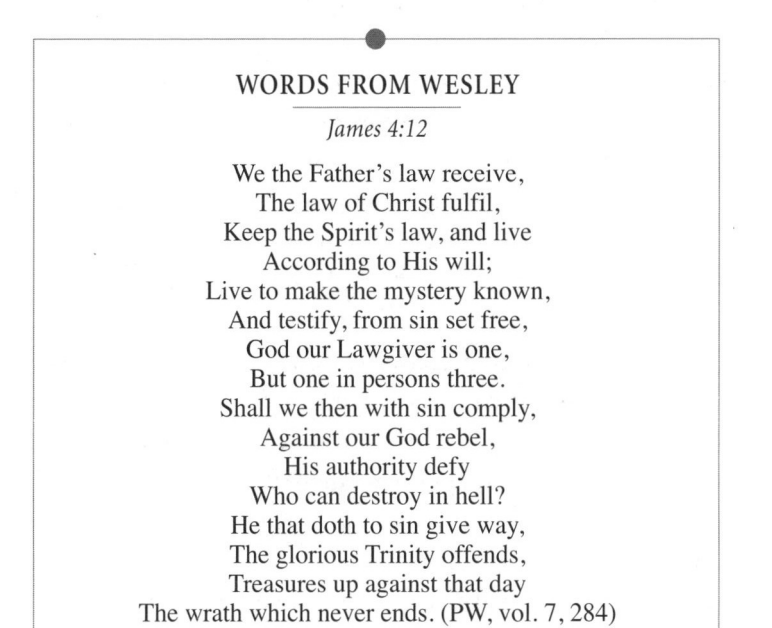

WORDS FROM WESLEY

James 4:12

We the Father's law receive,
The law of Christ fulfil,
Keep the Spirit's law, and live
According to His will;
Live to make the mystery known,
And testify, from sin set free,
God our Lawgiver is one,
But one in persons three.
Shall we then with sin comply,
Against our God rebel,
His authority defy
Who can destroy in hell?
He that doth to sin give way,
The glorious Trinity offends,
Treasures up against that day
The wrath which never ends. (PW, vol. 7, 284)

But you seem to have no fear of God's judgment. Stop and think for a moment. **Who are you to judge your neighbor?** (James 4:12). You aren't God. You are not your neighbor's master (see Rom. 14:4). In fact, you're not even smart enough to fear the only Lawgiver and Judge. Repent and submit to Him before it's too late. Remember, "Judgment without mercy will be shown to anyone who has not been merciful. [But] mercy triumphs over judgment!" (James 2:13).

Don't Ignore God (James 4:13–17)

Now listen, you who say, "Today or tomorrow we will go to this or that city, spend a year there, carry on business and make money" (v. 13). James appeared to be alarmed at the way these Christians were virtually ignoring God in the day-to-day matters of life. They ran their businesses without consulting God. They were living as though God didn't exist.

He confronted their "moral dementia" with two hard-hitting statements. First he said, **you do not even know what will happen tomorrow** (v. 14). In fact only God knows what will happen in the next minute. Solomon wrote similar words: "Do not boast about tomorrow, for you do not know what a day may bring forth" (Prov. 27:1). Just like slandering others reveals that a person thinks he or she is God's superior, so does planning that pretends to know the future.

But James wasn't finished. His second statement began with a question: **What is your life?** (James 4:14). What is the nature of your existence in this world? **You are a mist that appears for a little while and then vanishes** (v. 14). Humans are no more than small puffs of smoke that disappear almost as quickly as they appear. How can anyone who doesn't know what will happen tomorrow, and may not even live long enough to find out, act like he or she is superior to God? God knows the end from the beginning. He is eternal; we are not.

James then contrasted what Christians should do against what they shouldn't: **Instead, you ought to say, "If it is the Lord's will, we will live and do this or that"** (v. 15). The author of Proverbs knew the limitations of our plans long before James pointed them out. "In his heart a man plans his course, but the

LORD determines his steps" (Prov. 16:9). "Many are the plans in a man's heart, but it is the LORD's purpose that prevails" (Prov. 19:21). Christian planning always defers to God's will. After all, His choice is the one that will become reality. **As it is,** when you plan your life and ignore God, **you boast and brag** (James 4:16). You are pretending to be God and you're not. **All such boasting is evil** (v. 16). It will destroy your life. It will frustrate you because you will "want something but don't get it" (4:2). The only cure for this diseased way of living is to "submit yourselves . . . to God" (4:7). **Anyone, then, who knows the good he ought to do and doesn't do it, sins** (v. 17). That person's faith is dead (2:14–26).

●

WORDS FROM WESLEY

James 4:17

Therefore to him that knoweth to do good and doth it not—That knows what is right, and does not practise it, *to him it is sin*—His knowledge does not prevent, but increase his condemnation. (ENNT)

This closing verse is one of the biblical definitions of sin that impresses upon us the extent of God's holiness. Paul said, "Everything that does not come from faith is sin" (Rom. 14:23). And John said, "All wrongdoing is sin" (1 John 5:17). Christians submitted to God's will, will not separate the prohibitions of the Bible from its commands. If a believer tries to make that separation, he or she is judging the law and faces God's discipline. So, once a person knows the good he or she ought to do, he or she must do it. If one doesn't do it, one sins. There are no other options.

DISCUSSION

When we give our lives to God, we also give Him our dreams, our plans, and our schedules to shape them as He will.

1. James used an example from business to show the futility of counting on the future. What other examples might show our dependence on God?

2. Define *slander*.

3. What might have caused the Christians to whom James wrote to judge one another? What type of things cause Christians to judge one another today?

4. What is a grace-filled way to respond to someone who is judgmental?

5. Based on James' teaching, would you say Christians should *not* set goals? Why or why not?

6. Describe a situation that caused you to feel the uncertainty of life.

7. Can you recall a time you were misjudged? Share how it made you feel.

8. Would you describe God as your consultant, your boss, or a passenger in your life? Explain.

9. What is God's rightful place in your conversations? Your job? Your goals?

PRAYER

Father, help us to be spiritually discerning, while at the same time avoiding being judgmental. Amen.

THE PROBLEM WITH MONEY

James 5:1–6

Our use of wealth reveals the condition of our hearts.

Most people do not consider themselves to be rich. No matter how much we have, we tend to look over the fence or across town and think of the other person as "wealthy." Regardless of our income, however, we still recognize the uncertain nature of finances and material things. Sure, things may be good right now, but there'll be another mortgage payment due next month, the kids need braces, and the mileage on the car is getting a bit high. Though we have much, we always feel the need for more.

This study plays on that tension we feel about money—and what we must do to acquire it. You will be challenged to examine your life to ensure that your holiness does not end where your finances begin.

COMMENTARY

To understand James' words to the rich oppressors addressed in James 5, we must look back at chapter 4. James had been addressing those who were proud. They exalted themselves by relying on themselves rather than God. It was only the humble person, seeing that he was inadequate in himself, who was able to confess, repent, and come to a saving knowledge of Christ.

In the same way, it is only the humble Christian whose trust is in God, not in his or her own abilities, who can truly know God. Our confidence is not in our own ability to control our lives and destinies. Instead, we ought to say, "If it is the Lord's will, we will live and do this or that" (James 4:15). Our confidence is never in ourselves. It must be in our Lord and Savior, Jesus Christ. It is in this context that James turned the discussion toward riches.

Riches Destroyed (James 5:1–3)

James moved from addressing all classes of people to directing his instruction to a very specific group, the rich: **Weep and wail because of the misery that is coming upon you** (v. 1). He gave them full warning of the misery that awaited them. To **wail** here literally means to shriek or howl and carries with it the idea of frantic fear. Whatever constitutes this **misery**, it is reason enough to cause great fear.

●

WORDS FROM WESLEY
James 5:10

Come now, ye rich—The apostle does not speak this so much for the sake of the rich themselves, as of the poor children of God, who were then groaning under their cruel oppression. *Weep and howl for your miseries which are coming upon you*—Quickly and unexpectedly. This was written not long before the siege of Jerusalem; during which, as well as after it, huge calamities came on the Jewish nation, not only in Judea, but through distant countries. And as these were an awful prelude of that wrath which was to fall upon them in the world to come, so this may likewise refer to the final vengeance which will then be executed on the impenitent. (ENNT)

Wealth is a very temporary condition. When people have little financial security, they tend to equate riches with security. In many minds, wealth is a permanent condition: You either have it or you don't. If you have it, you have security. But that is a worldly view of money. The biblical view makes it very clear: Riches are temporary. Riches are destined for destruction. **Your**

wealth has rotted, and moths have eaten you clothes. Your gold and silver are corroded (vv. 2–3).

Wealth in the Near East was recognized in three forms: (1) produce, such as grain; (2) clothes; and (3) precious metals and stones. This is clearly seen in the experience of Gehazi, Elisha's servant. After Elisha had miraculously provided for Naaman's healing from leprosy, he refused Naaman's gifts. Gehazi was overcome by his desire for wealth, followed Naaman, and requested a talent of silver and two sets of clothing. The absurdity of the situation was that he would never be able to wear the clothes in public or else Elisha would know of his deception. But as it often is with riches, it's not the use of them as much as the intoxication of possessing them that causes a person's downfall. Gehazi's riches were in the form of clothes and silver, two of the very things mentioned by James. (See 2 Kings 5 for the whole story.)

We must ask the question, do gold and silver corrode? If our confidence was in gold and silver, and someone warned us that it would corrode, we would be quite smug in our belief that it would not. There are financial advisors today who suggest returning to the gold standard or at least investing in precious metals because of their permanence in value when compared to paper money. Even Paul used gold and silver as examples of what will not burn up on the day of judgment.

Rather than a literal view of this statement, it would benefit the reader to understand that the point is that even what appears to be durable to us is only temporary in an eternal economy. Even in earthly economic terms, gold and silver can lose their value. They may not literally corrode, but their value can dissolve. Compared to eternal things, silver and gold have no value.

Riches Turned against the Rich (James 5:3–6)

James claimed that our riches **will testify against** us (v. 3). Not only will the riches lose their value and benefit, they will also work against us! It is important to note that the problem here is not the riches themselves. God does not condemn those with wealth simply because they are wealthy. It is no more righteous to be poor than to be rich. These rich people had selfishness at the root of their wealth. Their downfall began with a selfishness that spawned many other sins. This truth is evidenced by the clarifications James used to explain the attaining of this wealth. The people James addressed **hoarded** (v. 3) their riches; they refused to **pay** earned **wages** (v. 4); they **lived** in **self-indulgence** (v. 5); and they **condemned and murdered innocent men** (v. 6). Those are some serious accusations against men who claimed allegiance to the teachings of the Scriptures. James condemned these people in no uncertain terms just as the Old Testament prophets denounced sin.

The latter part of verse 5 likens the self-indulgent to sheep being prepared for slaughter: **You have fattened yourselves in the day of slaughter.** The sheep is given as much as it wants to eat. Nothing is required of it that would expend energy and burn up fat. It is given a life of luxury. It gladly eats all it can, totally oblivious to the fact that all this is for its destruction. Those who spend their riches on themselves are doing the same thing. They think they are living in the lap of luxury, but that luxury has a deadly consequence. That luxury is preparing them for destruction.

God has always lent a sympathetic ear to the poor who have been treated unjustly. In this case, **the cries of the harvesters have reached the ears of the Lord Almighty** (v. 4). The day laborer in Palestine was barely able to eke out an existence. Withholding his wages for even one day meant that his family would be one step closer to starvation. James contrasted the poor, hardworking laborer with the calloused luxury of the self-indulgent rich man. Not only are they compared as being at opposite ends of the spectrum, they are interrelated as well. Those James addressed had gained their riches at the expense of the laborers. Consequently, the laborers experienced greater suffering because of the selfishness of the rich.

WORDS FROM WESLEY

James 5:4

The hire of your labourers crieth—Those sins chiefly cry to God, concerning which human laws are silent. Such are luxury, unchastity, and various kinds of injustice. The labourers themselves also cry to God, who is just coming to avenge their cause. (ENNT)

Many rich would claim innocence in regard to harming anyone by their attainment of riches. They have come by their wealth in an honest and upright manner. But even before James addressed dishonest gain, he condemned the hoarding of riches: **You have hoarded wealth in the last days** (v. 3). Hoarding what could have been used for the advancement of the kingdom of God is a symptom of love of money. No gift that comes from God is for our benefit alone. Everything He gives us is to be shared with others. What we hoard will testify against us.

You have lived on earth in luxury and self-indulgence (v. 5). One of the reasons Jesus said it was so hard for a rich man to enter the kingdom of heaven is because it is so easy for him to develop a lifestyle of self-indulgence. With riches comes opportunity for all the sensual pleasures of the world. **Self-indulgence**, as it is used here, infers a satisfying of one's own lusts. James was not referring to a wholesome pleasure derived from good things, such as being satisfied after a good meal. He was referring to a gratification gained through sinful lust. A person loses all perspective of the needs of a lost and dying world when all the pleasures of life are at his or her fingertips.

The Fate of the Rich (James 5:3)

James described the fate of those whose confidence lies in their riches. The **corrosion** of those riches will **eat your flesh**

like fire (v. 3). This description gives a twofold view of their condemnation. First, it can be interpreted as a destruction of the physical body here on earth. It is a common occurrence for a selfish attitude toward wealth to literally destroy one's health. Ulcers, cancer, and heart problems can all be caused by a heart that is self-centered and self-gratifying.

Second, it is clear that eternal damnation is a result of a life lived for self rather than God. Hell is an eternal flame that burns the flesh. Scripture describes hell in both physical and spiritual terms. The literal physical body decays and is left behind; therefore the flesh that covers our present bodies cannot experience the suffering of hell. Our spirits, which are eternal, will not just be vapors or ethereal beings. There will be resurrected bodies of some kind. Even those who are not resurrected to life but to eternal punishment will have some form of a physical body that will experience physical torment.

WORDS FROM WESLEY

James 5:6

Ye have killed the just—Many just men, in particular *that Just One* (Acts. 3:14). They afterward killed James, surnamed the Just, the writer of this epistle. *He doth not resist you*—And therefore you are secure. But the Lord cometh quickly, ver. 8. (ENNT)

DISCUSSION

The life of a disciple is inconsistent with the life of one who gains wealth, luxury, or convenience through the oppression of others.

1. Many Old Testament saints were men of wealth. Name a few.

2. What makes these Old Testament leaders different from the people James addressed?

3. What contemporary situations might incite James' indictment?

4. In what ways do you see the love of money affecting people in our culture? In what ways has this attraction affected you?

5. Money seems to create a moral blind spot for many people. Why do you think that is?

6. React to this statement: "The desire to gain wealth is always dangerous."

7. Have you ever observed someone cheating or harming another person for his or her own gain? How did it make you feel? Did you do anything about it?

8. What practical steps can we take to ensure that our desire for gain does not harm others?

9. What are you doing to guard your integrity?

PRAYER

Father, may we be good and generous stewards of the money with which You entrust us. Amen.

THE WISDOM OF PATIENCE

James 5:7–12

We must patiently endure in all circumstances until Christ returns.

One of the benefits of living in a modern society is the ability to control most aspects of life. We can adjust the temperature in our homes by turning a dial. When the television blares annoying advertisements, we dispatch them with the click of a button. We don't like inconvenience, and we seldom have to deal with it.

That can cause us to be impatient with circumstances we can't control, such as illness, broken relationships, or injustice. When we suffer problems for which there seems to be no solution, it can challenge both our patience and our faith. This study will give you the peace of mind to endure current circumstances with the confidence that Christ will resolve all things in the end.

COMMENTARY

The words James shared as he approached the end of this letter turn toward the second coming of Christ. James did not attempt to present any doctrine concerning how the second coming will take place or even how to recognize the signs of Christ's coming. Instead, James, as has been characteristic of the entire letter, was most concerned about the practical Christian life of believers as they await the second coming of Christ. He returned to this subject, which he addressed earlier in the letter (James 1:3–4).

Patience (James 5:7–9)

Be patient, then, brothers, until the Lord's coming. . . . You too, be patient (vv. 7–8). Twice in this section we are exhorted to be patient. The double command emphasizes our tremendous need of this grace. Many opportunities for service and privilege have been lost because we are not willing to patiently wait on God's timing. Impatience, all too often, keeps us from submission to God's will.

There are two kinds of patience. One is a patience that is inactive, if not lethargic. It sits back and waits, not with activity or responsibility, but with a *laissez-faire* attitude that is almost fatalistic. It is a patience that borders on laziness, waiting for God to make the next move. It says, "What will be will be. I can't change the future, so I'll sit back and do nothing until fate overtakes me."

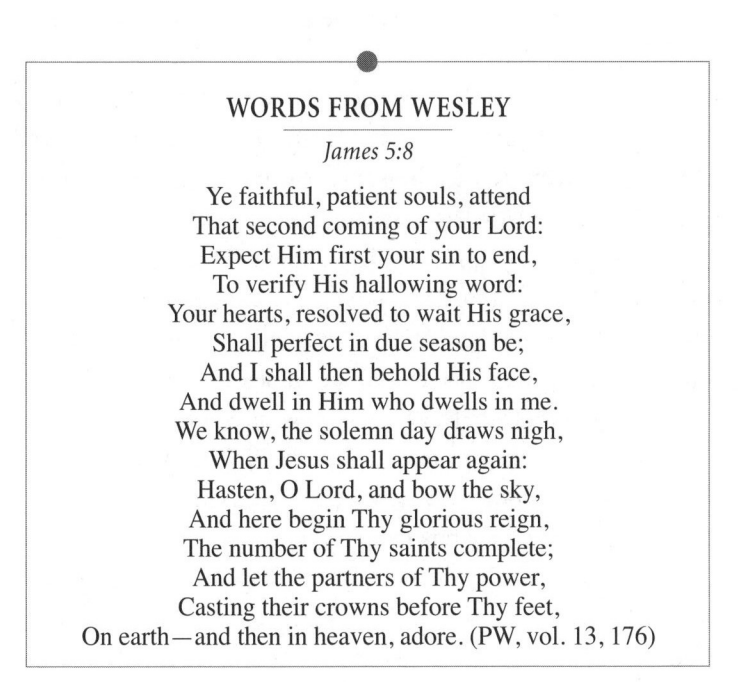

WORDS FROM WESLEY

James 5:8

Ye faithful, patient souls, attend
That second coming of your Lord:
Expect Him first your sin to end,
To verify His hallowing word:
Your hearts, resolved to wait His grace,
Shall perfect in due season be;
And I shall then behold His face,
And dwell in Him who dwells in me.
We know, the solemn day draws nigh,
When Jesus shall appear again:
Hasten, O Lord, and bow the sky,
And here begin Thy glorious reign,
The number of Thy saints complete;
And let the partners of Thy power,
Casting their crowns before Thy feet,
On earth—and then in heaven, adore. (PW, vol. 13, 176)

In contrast, there is a second kind of patience. It is a patience like that of **the farmer** (v. 7). He has worked hard planting and cultivating his crop. He does not sit back and expect God to do the work. He has done all he can to ensure a successful harvest, but he also knows that until it is time to harvest the crop, he must wait and trust God to send the rain and produce the yield. This is a patience, absent of worry, that exercises faith and trust in God. As we wait for the Lord's coming, we are to actively work in our fields of service, yet patiently understand that the fruits of our labors are totally in God's hands.

Much better than the example of the farmer is the example of God himself. Because of His desire to see us saved, He waits patiently and continues to offer salvation to all who will believe. His return is delayed until every opportunity for salvation is given, until all men and women who will respond have been given opportunity to do so. His patience is a gracious act of love.

Along with patience is the admonition to **stand firm** (v. 8). Don't give up, get careless, or become fearful during the waiting process. This instruction to stand firm was a familiar command to Jewish readers. It was the same instruction given by Moses to the children of Israel as they stood on the edge of the Red Sea with Pharaoh's army pressing in on them. They were terrified, crying out to Moses in fear. Moses' response was, "Do not be afraid. Stand firm and you will see the deliverance the LORD will bring you today" (Ex. 14:13). Since James was addressing predominantly Jewish believers, they would recognize and be encouraged by this command. The same God who delivered Moses and the children of Israel will deliver us from suffering and persecution. Our job is to stand firm.

The Lord's coming is near (v. 8). The early believers fully expected Christ's return to be immediate, at least within their lifetime. James was not concerned with timelines, charts, and the order of events surrounding Christ's second coming. It was not something to analyze. The Lord's return was something to expect at any moment. It was a great encouragement to the people to whom James wrote that their persecutions could soon come to an end by Christ's return. Whenever the church of Jesus Christ loses sight of His imminent return, it loses its vitality. **Don't grumble against each other, brothers** (v. 9). It is easy for believers to begin grumbling when they are waiting on God. **Grumbling** here is complaining or criticizing, similar to that done by the children of Israel as they murmured against Moses. It displays itself most often as "blaming" and is generally directed at others. This critical spirit is usually not focused on the fact that Christ's coming has not taken place according to our expectations. Rather, it is focused on the many things about our lives and the lives of others that we don't like. Grumbling takes place, all too often, during the process of waiting.

Blaming, criticizing, and murmuring against others are acts of judgment. You and I are not to exercise judgment against others. We are reminded that the Lord's coming is near. With His coming comes judgment. He will make all things right, and He is the only One capable of bringing judgment. Be assured His judgment will be brought against those who grumble against each other.

Examples of Patience (James 5:10–11)

James instructed his readers to look at the **prophets** as **an example of patience in the face of suffering** (v. 10). There is no biblical guarantee that the road of life will be easy. Suffering and persecution were common characteristics of life for the first-century Christian. Patience is a virtue during times of ease; it is a lifesaver in times of suffering.

The prophets **spoke in the name of the Lord** (v. 10). They did not speak of their own accord, but at God's direct command. Even though they suffered because of the message they presented, they **persevered** (v. 11). Patience often carries the need for perseverance. Perseverance is the act of continuing on in spite of opposition.

WORDS FROM WESLEY
James 5:10

Take the prophets for an example—Once persecuted like you, even for *speaking in the name of the Lord*—The very men that gloried in having prophets, yet could not bear their message. Nor did either their holiness, or their high commission screen them from suffering. (ENNT)

The prophets suffered in a manner that is most difficult to accept. They were persecuted by the very people to whom they were ministering. It would be understandable if they suffered at the hands of Israel's enemies; instead, it was the people of Israel who rejected, ridiculed, and opposed their preaching. In the midst of this injustice, however, they were patient. Their patience was characterized by a trust in God to bring everything to justice and judgment. The greatest honor given by God was reserved for those who suffered most. **As you know, we consider blessed those who have persevered** (v. 11). Follow their example when criticism assails you.

You have heard of Job's perseverance. We are not the first ones to face suffering; neither are we the first ones to exhibit patience. Job is given as another example of one who suffered greatly but showed patience (v. 11). If he was able to endure in spite of his immense suffering, there is reason to believe that we can as well.

As is often a person's response, Job could not understand the suffering that God allowed him to endure. Job's suffering affected several areas of his life. He suffered material loss; his wealth, flocks, and herds were simultaneously destroyed. He endured the unspeakable grief of the death of all his children at once by what appeared to be a mysterious and senseless natural calamity. His body was wracked with terrible physical pain. Faced with mental agony while wrestling with accusations and advice of wife and friends, never had anyone suffered as greatly as Job. Despite these traumas, Job remained faithful in his commitment to God. Even at the coaxing of friends and family, he refused to turn his back on God.

Job's patience was exhibited by faithfulness, but there were other characteristics displayed by Job that did not appear to be acts of patience. There are those whose personalities are quite placid. Patience seems to come quite naturally for them. Job does not appear to be among those with a calm, accepting temperament. It was not his nature to be patient. During his suffering, he constantly challenged God with the question, "Why?" He did not passively accept his situation, but he hounded God for an explanation. His patience was not displayed in passivity but in holding on to God no matter what the circumstances. Patience is not the absence of questioning or frustration with God but perseverance in spite of the unanswered questions. Feelings of indignation did not keep Job from being an example of patience.

Interestingly, God never felt it necessary to give Job an explanation; instead, He gave Job a greater revelation of himself. What the Lord finally brought about for Job was commendation before his accusing friends and a restoration of all Job had lost — and more! Satan did not triumph over Job. Among other things, God reveals His **compassion and mercy** (v. 11) in the midst of suffering. The Lord was with Job in his suffering, exerting His hand of control over Satan and the afflictions that came against Job. God blessed Job in the midst of suffering, and ironically, because of his suffering, we have the example of Job's patience. If he had only prospered, we would never know of his patience.

.

A common view of the Jewish people was that the Messiah would come with a sword in judgment. When Christ came in peace, preaching a message of love, many rejected Him. His second coming will be one of judgment, but even that judgment is characterized by **compassion and mercy** (v. 11). The patience of God in refraining from returning is a great example of His love and compassion.

Do Not Swear (James 5:12)

There is no apparent reason why verse 12 is placed in the context of patience regarding the Lord's return. It may be just a valuable piece of advice that stands on its own and came to the mind of the writer as he was preparing to close the letter.

The meaning of **swear** must be made plain. James did not address any attempt to take the Lord's name in vain. **Swear** in this passage refers to making an oath in order to prove the sincerity and truth of the statement. A Christian's word should be credible without needing further oaths.

●

WORDS FROM WESLEY
James 5:12

Swear not—However provoked. The Jews were notoriously guilty of common swearing, though not so much by God himself as by some of His creatures. The apostle here particularly forbids these oaths, as well as all swearing in common conversation. It is very observable how solemnly the apostle introduces this command: *above all things, swear not.* As if he had said, Whatever you forget, do not forget this. This abundantly demonstrates the horrible iniquity of the crime. But he does not forbid the taking of a solemn oath before a magistrate. *Let your yea be yea, and your nay nay*—Use no higher asseverations in common discourse. And let your word stand firm. Whatever ye say, take care to make it good. (ENNT)

The Jews were known to exercise a common swearing upon various objects (for example, heaven, earth, Jerusalem, the temple, the altar). It required an informed person to know what was considered binding and what was not. Jesus, as well as James, condemned such deception. The Christian is to be completely honest. There should be no variations of intent or subtle incongruities. **Let your "Yes" be yes, and your "No," no** (v. 12). If we must swear an oath to prove our honesty, we are not people of integrity. A person who lies in common conversation is a liar and will lie while taking an oath as well.

DISCUSSION

Patience is a fruit of the Spirit that rises out of our faith in God and hope that we trust will never disappoint us.

1. Would you agree that patience is the most difficult of all virtues to acquire? Why or why not?

2. James used a farmer as an example of patience. What other situations might be good examples of patience?

3. Why should we be patient?

4. James seems to address Christians who had begun to quarrel. What kinds of situations cause Christians to become annoyed with one another?

5. What advice do you think James would give to a church that was experiencing tension or divisions?

6. James advised us to say what we mean and mean what we say. List some reasons why that is important for Christians to do.

7. James mentioned Old Testament heroes who displayed patience. Can you give examples of contemporary saints who displayed patience?

8. Does thinking about the return of Christ make you feel impatient, optimistic, frustrated, or none of the above? Why?

9. What is the greatest challenge you face in anticipating the return of Christ?

10. What can you do to prepare yourself for Christ's return?

PRAYER

Father, may we plan as if Your Son is not returning for another hundred years and live as if He is returning today. Amen.

THE POWER OF PRAYER

James 5:13–20

Our ability to pray ensures that we will never be helpless.

Does prayer work? Most of us would say yes without giving the question much thought. We know what the "right" answer is. But when we face an intractable illness, a broken relationship, or a personal tragedy and pray repeatedly for God's intervention yet see no result, we may come back to that nagging question, "What is the value of prayer?"

Knowing that all believing people will face this problem sooner or later, James addressed it head-on in his letter. Without apology, he offered the straightforward advice that we should pray with confidence for healing. Why? Because prayer works. This study will boost your confidence in the power of prayer and cause you to seek God's help for the problems you face.

COMMENTARY

It is fitting that such a practical epistle about living the Christian life end with a discourse on prayer. Prayer is one of the foundation stones of the Christian life.

Tradition tells us that James' knees were compared to those of a camel—rough and callused because of time spent on his knees in prayer. Words become more powerful when they are supported by a man who practiced what he preached.

Pray in Trouble and in Joy (James 5:13)

Is any one of you in trouble? He should pray. Is anyone happy? Let him sing songs of praise (v. 13). Immediately, James proposed two times when prayer is a necessity: in trouble and in joy. More than simply addressing two isolated occasions, the intent is obvious that prayer fits both these occasions and all others in between.

It is the privilege of the believer to go to God in prayer when faced with trouble. The command to pray here is not limited to any particular kind of trouble. Whatever trouble one finds oneself in, it is an opportunity to pray. God is concerned about everything that troubles us and does not intend for us to carry the burden of trouble alone. As we bring our burdens to Him in prayer, He is able to answer our prayer and lighten the burden. It is also during times of affliction that we are humbly aware of our tremendous need for God.

A vital part of being created in the image of God is that we have emotions just like Him. God is not only there for us in times of trouble but also in times of joy. Singing **songs of praise** is the appropriate response to happiness. God has provided our happiness, and it needs to be expressed back to Him. The quality of our singing voice has little to do with praise in song. We are conditioned to hearing public singing of high quality, but there is nothing more lovely than praise coming from the heart intended for God's benefit, not for the benefit of a human audience. A clear evidence of a joyful congregation is the exuberance expressed when singing praise to God. Worship music lacking the emotion of joy is less than attractive to anyone. Praise is the highest form of prayer.

Pray for Physical Healing (James 5:14–15)

God gives a clear command to the sick. **He should call the elders of the church to pray over him and anoint him with**

oil in the name of the Lord (v. 14). Given the poor medical treatment of the day, this command is understandable. Prayer was the only recourse and hope of recovery for Christians in the first century. With advances in medical technology of the present day, many illnesses that were potentially fatal then are now of little concern. Consequently, prayer often becomes a plan of action only when medical treatment fails. But prayer should be the first response of the Christian. We should be more dependent on God than on the doctor.

WORDS FROM WESLEY

James 5:14

Having anointed him with oil—This single, conspicuous gift, which Christ committed to His apostles (Mark 6:13), remained in the church long after the other miraculous gifts were withdrawn. Indeed it seems to have been designed to remain always, and St. James directs the elders, who were the most, if not the only gifted men, to administer it. This was the whole process of physic in the Christian church, till it was lost through unbelief. (ENNT)

The elders of the church (v. 14) should become involved with those who are sick. The sick are not just to call out to God, but they are to look to the elders of the church to pray with them. One of the joys of the Christian life is the community of believers; no one must suffer alone. The body of believers supports, encourages, and prays for each other. Turning to God does not mean we foolishly ignore medical treatment.

There is some evidence that the anointing oil used at this time was purely a medicinal treatment rather than a spiritual symbol. It was characteristic of early Christians to care for the sick. If the anointing with oil was medicinal in nature, then this verse presents a valid case for combining medical technology with spiritual dependence on God. Prayer for the sick is not commanded as a placebo, but it is clear that **the prayer offered in faith will make the sick person well** (v. 15). It is the responsibility of the sick person to contact the elders and request prayer and anointing. There are always those in the church who expect the elders to invite themselves to the laying on of hands. Certainly prayer can be given on behalf of the sick without their request, but the laying on of hands and anointing with oil are clearly to be at the request of the sick. Once that request is made, it is the responsibility of the elders to respond accordingly. The healing is always a work of God. The elders pray in the name of the Lord.

This promise should not be used as a guarantee that God will always heal—if we have enough faith. Too many Christians have placed blame upon themselves when a healing did not take place, assuming that their faith was weak. This passage must be kept in balance with all of Scripture. Often God will heal, but if physical healing is not in the best eternal interest of the individual, healing does not always take place.

Pray for Spiritual Healing (James 5:15–16)

It is not by accident that James immediately moved from physical healing to the forgiveness of sins. **If he has sinned, he will be forgiven** (v. 15). Jesus was interested in physical healing, but He was even more concerned with spiritual healing. Often, before healing someone physically, He would heal them spiritually by saying, "Your sins are forgiven." He came first to redeem sinners and forgive sins. Physical healing is valuable only as it leads to spiritual healing. Prayer is the avenue for forgiveness of sins. There is no other remedy for sin, other than confession and repentance.

Therefore confess your sins to each other and pray for each other so that you may be healed (v. 16). Prayer combined with confession also brings healing to broken relationships among believers. The purpose of confession is reconciliation and healing. Any confession that does not move toward that end is inappropriate. The *Beacon Bible Expositions* helps us understand proper confession: "Secret sins should be confessed specifically to God alone. Sins against persons should be confessed to those persons, as far as this is possible. Public sins should be publicly confessed." James' command of verse 16 is seldom heeded by Christians. Many divisions exist in the church today because Christians are hesitant to admit their offenses to each other.

WORDS FROM WESLEY

James 5:16

In the evening three women agreed to meet together weekly, with the same intention as those at London—viz. 'to confess their faults one to another, and pray one for another, that they may be healed.' At eight four young men agreed to meet, in pursuance of the same design. How dare any man deny this to be (as to the substance of it) a means of grace, ordained by God? Unless he will affirm (with Luther in the fury of his Solifidianism ["faith alone"]) that St. James' epistle is an epistle of straw. (JJW, vol. 2, 174)

The Power of Prayer (James 5:16–18)

The only qualification given to the one praying is that **the prayer of a *righteous* man is powerful and effective** (v. 16, emphasis added). Only one whose sins are forgiven and who is in right standing with God can claim power in prayer. "If I had cherished sin in my heart, the Lord would not have listened" (Ps. 66:18).

Elijah (James 5:17) is cited as an example of a righteous man who experienced the power of prayer. Although he was nothing more than **a man just like us**, he was able to change weather patterns by prayer alone. There is no doubt God was the source of Elijah's power. It was not the power of Elijah that was able to stop and start the rain. There is also no doubt that Elijah was the instrument God used to accomplish the miracle. Elijah's prayers were the channels God used to accomplish His will. It is still the same today: **The prayer of a righteous man is powerful and effective** (v. 16).

It must be noted that **Elijah . . . prayed earnestly** (v. 17). Often our prayers are without passion. It's not that we don't mean what we pray; it is just that our entire selves are not thrown into the prayer. We want the answer, but we don't want it desperately enough. We pray as if it doesn't matter whether God answers the prayer or not; this is not earnest prayer.

Spiritual Restoration (James 5:19–20)

James clearly stated the possibility of wandering from the truth. For us to be responsible as moral agents, we must have free will. Each person is responsible for his or her own actions, choices, and decisions. Wandering is a choice of the individual, not something that befalls a person without his or her consent. **The error of his way** (v. 20) refers to free choice. This **error** is not an unintentional mistake. It is a voluntary act of misconduct.

It is the responsibility of the believers to do everything in our power to **bring him back** (v. 19). Our discomfort in confronting someone about his or her spiritual wandering is more than surpassed by the joy of saving someone from spiritual death. The salvation of souls is the greatest work in which the believer can participate, but keep in mind that we are only participants. No person can convert another. Even God has chosen to limit himself in that He will not convert a sinner apart from the free will of the sinner him- or herself. As we labor together with God for the conversion of sinners, each person remains accountable to God for his or her own choices.

WORDS FROM WESLEY

James 5:19

As if he had said, I have now warned you of those sins, to which you are most liable. And in all these respects watch not only over yourselves, but every one over his brother also. Labour in particular to recover those that are fallen. *If any one err from the truth*—Practically by sin. (ENNT)

When the sinner's sins are forgiven by turning to God in repentance, God will **cover over a multitude of sins** (v. 20). God fulfills His promise to forgive us when we confess our sins to Him (see 1 John 1:9). We need to make sure our personal life is right before God and encourage others to do the same.

DISCUSSION

Part of the way we learn faith, trust, and hope is by investing our hearts and lives in prayer.

1. Describe the specific steps James listed in this passage concerning prayer for healing.

2. What is the relationship between confession and healing?

3. Elijah is used as a biblical example of effective prayer. What other examples can you name?

4. Do you think James' instructions are meant to preclude the use of modern medicine? Why or why not?

5. Can you think of other Bible verses or stories where Jesus commended someone for his or her faith?

6. Why does prayer so often seem to be a last resort for Christians?

7. Do you believe miracles still occur? Explain.

8. Have you ever helped to "turn a sinner from the error of his or her way"? Without revealing incriminating details, tell about the change you saw in the person's life as a result.

9. What are some ways we can draw near to God?

PRAYER

Our Father in heaven, hallowed be Your name, Your kingdom come, Your will be done on earth as it is in heaven. Amen.

WORDS FROM WESLEY WORKS CITED

ENNT: *Explanatory Notes upon the New Testament,* by John Wesley, M.A. Fourth American Edition. New York: J. Soule and T. Mason, for the Methodist Episcopal Church in the United States, 1818.

JJW: *The Journal of the Rev. John Wesley, A.M.* Standard. Edited by Nehemiah Curnock. 8 vols. London: Robert Culley, Charles H. Kelley, 1909–1916.

PW: *The Poetical Works of John and Charles Wesley.* Edited by D. D. G. Osborn. 13 vols. London: Wesleyan-Methodist Conference Office, 1868.

WJW: *The Works of John Wesley.* Third Edition, Complete and Unabridged. 14 vols. London: Wesleyan Methodist Book Room, 1872.

OTHER BOOKS IN THE
WESLEY BIBLE STUDIES SERIES

Genesis (available February 2015)
Exodus (available April 2015)
Leviticus through Deuteronomy (available June 2015)
Joshua through Ruth (available June 2015)
1 Samuel through 2 Chronicles (available February 2015)
Ezra through Esther (available April 2015)
Job through Song of Songs (available February 2015)
Isaiah (available April 2015)
Jeremiah through Daniel (available February 2015)
Hosea through Malachi (available June 2015)
Matthew
Mark
Luke (available September 2014)
John (available April 2014)
Acts (available September 2014)
Romans (available June 2014)
1–2 Corinthians (available September 2014)
Galatians through Colossians and Philemon (available June 2014)
1–2 Thessalonians (available September 2014)
1 Timothy through Titus (available April 2014)
Hebrews (available April 2014)
James
1–2 Peter and Jude (available April 2014)
1–3 John (available June 2014)
Revelation (available June 2014)

Now Available in the Wesley Bible Studies Series

Each book in the Wesley Bible Studies series provides a thoughtful and powerful survey of key Scriptures in one or more biblical books. They combine accessible commentary from contemporary teachers, with relevantly highlighted direct quotes from the complete writings and life experiences of John Wesley, along with the poetry and hymns of his brother Charles. For each study, creative and engaging questions and activities likewise foster deeper fellowship and growth.

Matthew
978-0-89827-862-0
978-0-89827-863-7 (e-book)

Mark
978-0-89827-838-5
978-0-89827-839-2 (e-book)

wphonline.com
1.800.493.7539